FLAS

C000158057

The Flashback
European Ethnological Research Centre,
c/o the National Museums of Scotland,
Queen Street, Edinburgh EH2 1JD.

General Editor: Alexander Fenton

YOUR FATHER AND I

A Family's Story

told by

Isabella G MacLean

in letters edited and introduced by

Colin MacLean

Tuckwell Press
in association with
The European Ethnological Research Centre

First published in Great Britain in 1998 by
Tuckwell Press
The Mill House
Phantassie
East Linton
East Lothian EH40 3DG
Scotland

Thanks go to the Scotland Inheritance Fund
for financial support in the publication
of this volume

British Library Cataloguing-in-Publication Data
A Catalogue record for this book
is available on request from the
British Library

Typeset by Hewer Text Ltd, Edinburgh
Printed and bound by Cromwell Press, Trowbridge, Wiltshire

CONTENTS

FOREWORD

This volume, the sixth in the Flashback Series of the European Ethnological Research Centre, breaks new ground in two ways. Firstly, it takes the form of a series of letters from mother to son, in which the history of the family, including the nineteenth-century ancestry, is consciously explored and the actors contextualised. Secondly, it relates to a family whose members were for the most part imbued with a strong sense of religion. The unfolding of the story brings it right into the heart of what has been considered a major sector of Scottish identity – the almost overpowering presence of teh church, whether of the more extreme evangelical variety or the more conservative Auld Kirk or the breakaway Free Kirk. It paints a canvas of the times, roughly from the Disruption of 1843 to the time of the death of Colin's father, the Reverend Alexander MacLean, in 1932.

What creates the sense of god in mankind is a big question. It can be so strong as to constitute extreme fanaticism and blindness; it can be a guide to an upright way of living, in a spirit of christian tolerance. The same faith can be practised by people as different in character as were Isabella MacLean's father and mother. These letters do not give answers to the great whats and whys, but they present an extraordinarily well-observed picture of the thoughts and actions of related individuals, in Aberdeen, Cromarty, Glasgow and elsewhere, as they were affected by religion, by each other, by the First World War. Isabella, with her enviable gift of total recall, brings to life her characters through reminiscence, anecdote and shrewd noting of peculiarities. Colin encouraged her, perhaps driven by a wish to know better a father whom he lost at the age of seven. The result is a study from the inside of a family in which a strong sense of religious vocation was almost inevitable, and through these letters the consequences for the family of such dedication become clear. Acceptance of the hardships thereby caused includes financial stringency and the strong supporting role that a church wife was bound to play. There are the general attitudes of the family as part of a wider, similarly dedicated sector of the population, with forms of communication that often involve the relation of characterising anecdotes. In these and many other ways there are brought to light the thoughts and actions of a well defined but not easily classifiable group. These letters and Colin's added notes go a long way towards illuminating, in fine prose, the essential role played by the men of the cloth and their families in the everyday and spiritual life of the people of Scotland.

Alexander Fenton

PREFACE

My mother and I wrote to one another, usually twice a week, over some 16 years, first during the four years (1943–47) when I was a radar mechanic in the Royal Air Force, more than two years of my service being in Libya; second, after I graduated from Aberdeen University in 1950. I worked as a journalist for ten years in Glasgow, and then in London for five years, our correspondence ending in June of 1963 when my mother died.

I greatly regret that I did not keep the letters Mother wrote to me in the years '43 to '47. They would have provided a noteworthy account of life during and after the war, as well as an indication of my mother's thoughts and attitudes at that time. I failed to preserve the letters she sent me in the early 1950s. But then I decided that I should record as much as possible of her recollections of family and social life, this partly for family, partly for professional reasons (articles by myself which were published in the *Glasgow Herald* and *The Times* in the 1960s drew heavily on information from Mother's letters, as did a television programme on the 1843 Disruption and my family which was broadcast by the BBC in Scotland in the early 1970s). By the mid-1950s, for the first time in her life, Mother had time on her hands, so we agreed that she would write down what she could remember, sometimes merely by incorporating her reminiscences in letters. Having heard some of her family stories many times, I prompted her to tell about this and that person or event or institution, and I asked then for elaboration or evidence. By this time I was kicking myself for not having kept all or most of her letters, for by then I fully appreciated how exceptional was her memory and also how unusual was her talent as a letter-writer.

It was by then a talent which she needed to exercise. In one letter she referred to a newspaper report of a doctor saying that neighbours' chats 'at the closemouth or stairheid' were the best safeguard against mental disturbance: they got their minds relieved and didn't need a psychiatrist. 'I agree with him,' she wrote, 'only having no neighbours now and no close-mouth I find a letter does instead.' By this time she lived with my psychiatrist sister Helen in a comparatively isolated house in the grounds of Aberdeen's Mental Hospital.

Mother's letters always began 'My dear Colin' and were signed 'Your loving mother, Isabella G MacLean'. They were written, always on blue writing paper, with a J pen nib and ink, until illness in the 1960s made necessary the use of ballpoints, which she thought 'make my writing most unimpressive'. Returning in the mid-'90s to Mother's letters, now that retirement allows me time to pay them due attention, I appreciate especially the extent to which the custom and the art of letter-writing have disappeared from our lives - or, as would now be said, from our culture.

The material in this book comprises a number of set pieces she wrote about family and places and people and experiences. All of these have been amplified from Mother's replies to questions or from the free-flow of reminiscences which came as readily in her hundreds of letters as in her daily talk. To this free-flow our family had become accustomed over the years, realising only as we grew up that not all mothers talked - and could write - with her fluency and remarkable recall. Here and there I have (in brackets) inserted a few words of explanation or elaboration, some of these from notes I made after speaking to her. In the process of assembling what follows I have often regretted that I did not prompt her to write more, not least about the family's ten years in Glasgow. I had heard her speak a lot about that period but much of the detail has slipped from my own less retentive memory.

One of her daughters-in-law dared to wonder whether Mother invented or generously coloured her stories, especially about our Mid Stocket aunts; to which Mother replied that she was incapable of imagining things - 'I have absolutely no inventive ability, only complete recall'. There was at least one time, however, when her recall was temporarily suspended (p131).

The memories recorded by my mother in the 1950s and early 1960s were principally about years before I was born, in 1925, and much of what she told drew on the Saturday morning meetings with her grandmother in Lilybank Place and then Mid Stocket Road at the turn of the century, and also on extended family chat in a time long before radio, television etc came to turn interests outward and to threaten the survival of family conversation. My father died in Dingwall at the age of 52 in 1932, leaving Mother with five of a family, aged seven to twenty. My oldest sister was a medical student at Aberdeen University. It is convenient and appropriate to end Mother's story around that time. The people she describes have all passed on, and even descendants must be sufficiently distanced from those mentioned that no personal sensitivity should be aroused.

I offer a Postscript, about the events of 1932 and about their impact on my mother, but I do not here attempt a portrait of her to match her own portrayal of her parents, or of my father, or indeed of the many characters who make up the chequered pattern of one distinctive sector of Scottish life in the late nineteenth and early twentieth century.

Colin MacLean

Your Father and I

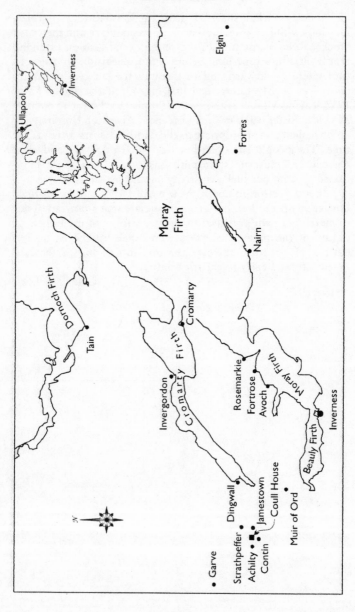

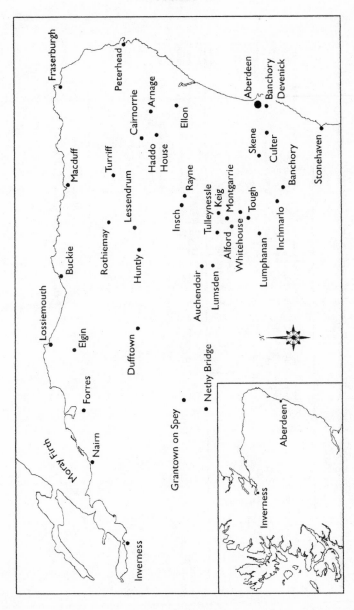

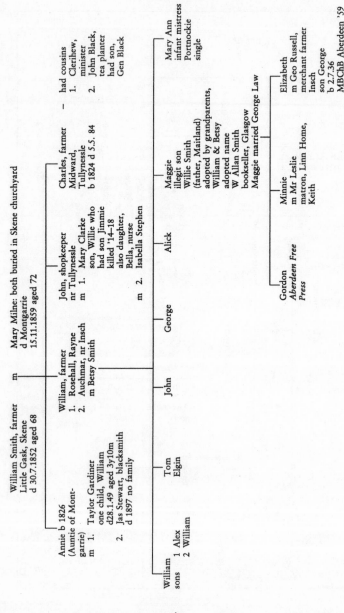

William Smith, farmer
Little Gask, Skene
d 30.7.1852 aged 68

m

Mary Milne: both buried in Skene churchyard
d Montgarrie
15.11.1859 aged 72

– had cousins
1. Clerihew,
   minister
2. John Black,
   tea planter
   had son,
   Gen Black

Annie b 1826
(Auntie of Mont-
garrie)
m 1. Taylor Gardiner
      one child, William
      d28.1.49 aged 3y10m
   2. Jas Stewart, blacksmith
      d 1897 no family

William, farmer
1. Rosehall, Rayne
2. Auchmar, nr Insch
m Betsy Smith

John, shopkeeper
nr Tullynessle
m 1. Mary Clarke
      who had son Jimmie
      killed '14–18
      also daughter,
      Bella, nurse
   2. Isabella Stephen

Charles, farmer
Midward,
Tullynessle
b 1824 d 5.5. 84

Mary Ann
infant mistress
Portnockie
single

William
sons 1 Alex
     2 William

Tom
Elgin

John

George

Alick

Maggie
illegit son
Willie Smith
(father, Maitland)
adopted by grandparents,
William & Betsy
adopted name
W Allan Smith
bookseller, Glasgow
Maggie married George Law

Gordon
*Aberdeen Free
Press*

Minnie
m Mr Leslie
matron, Linn Home,
Keith

Elizabeth
m Geo Russell,
merchant farmer
Insch
son George
b 2.7.36
MBChB Aberdeen '59

Preface

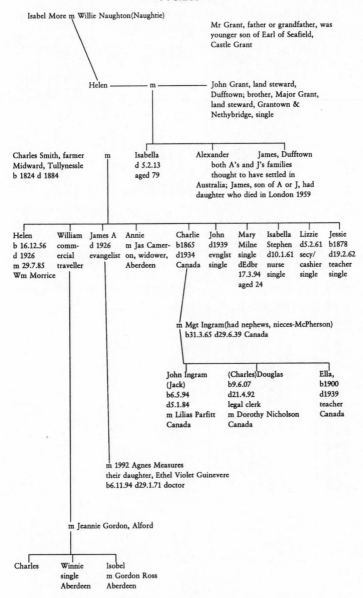

Isabel More m Willie Naughton(Naughtie)

Mr Grant, father or grandfather, was younger son of Earl of Seafield, Castle Grant

Helen ———— m ————— John Grant, land steward, Dufftown; brother, Major Grant, land steward, Grantown & Nethybridge, single

Charles Smith, farmer Midward, Tullynessle b 1824 d 1884 — m

Isabella d 5.2.13 aged 79

Alexander — James, Dufftown both A's and J's families thought to have settled in Australia; James, son of A or J, had daughter who died in London 1959

Helen b 16.12.56 d 1926 m 29.7.85 Wm Morrice

William commercial traveller

James A d 1926 evangelist

Annie m Jas Cameron, widower, Aberdeen

Charlie b1865 d1934 Canada

John d1939 evnglst single

Mary Milne single dEdbr 17.3.94 aged 24

Isabella Stephen d10.1.61 nurse single

Lizzie d5.2.61 secy/ cashier single

Jessie b1878 d19.2.62 teacher single

m Mgt Ingram(had nephews, nieces-McPherson) b31.3.65 d29.6.39 Canada

John Ingram (Jack) b6.5.94 d5.1.84 m Lilias Parfitt Canada

(Charles)Douglas b9.6.07 d21.4.92 legal clerk m Dorothy Nicholson Canada

Ella, b1900 d1939 teacher Canada

m 1992 Agnes Measures their daughter, Ethel Violet Guinevere b6.11.94 d29.1.71 doctor

m Jeannie Gordon, Alford

Charles

Winnie single Aberdeen

Isobel m Gordon Ross Aberdeen

I

BARE LIVING, HIGH THINKING

My grandfather Charles Smith was born in 1824 and died in 1884. He was the youngest son of William Smith and his wife Mary Milne, who are buried in the churchyard in Skene. His father was a farmer.

Charles had two brothers and one sister, all of whom belong to the family story. William was farmer at Rosehall, Rayne when my mother was young, and afterwards at Auchmar near Insch. John had a merchant's shop near Tullynessle. The sister, Annie, Mrs James Stewart, lived at Montgarrie, two miles from Tully-nessle on the one side and from Alford on the other. Her husband was the blacksmith there – no family.

Charles had the farm of Midward at Tullynessle and married Isabella Grant of Dufftown. My mother was their first child and was born in 1856. There were ten children, Helen, Willie, James, Annie, Charlie, John, Mary, Isa, Lizzie and Jessie.

Charles' brother William had five sons, William, Tom, John, George and Alick, and two daughters, Maggie, Mrs Law, and Mary Ann who was infants' mistress at Portnockie. William married the daughter of a well-to-do farmer – Aunt Betsy, they called her – named Smith also. Her brothers were very eccentric which perhaps accounted for the fact that all the Rosehall family had an odd simplicity of manner which didn't prevent them from being very fine people and from making a good deal of money.

Charles' other brother, John, was a silent sarcastic kind of man, not very lovable, but a model of honesty and integrity. His only child was Willie, father of Bella Smith, home-sister at Woodend. Willie's mother, Mary Clarke, had died of TB shortly after his birth. Mary Clarke had been employed as nurse for William Robertson Smith as a baby (see below). Willie had been christened in the same robe as WRS: it was made in a zenana in India. The robe is now (1961) in the possession of this family. It was passed to my mother and then to me. Mother never used it because none of our family was christened. Apart from some of the embroidery the robe is perished and discoloured with age.

When Willie Smith was left motherless, Auntie of Montgarrie took charge of him till his father married again. He was her favourite nephew and she always referred to him as 'my dear Willie'. Perhaps for that reason he was no great favourite with any of his cousins, except my mother who was extraordinarily kind to him and his family. John's second wife was Isabella Stephen, sister of the Alford banker. I remember her as a dignified old lady, so John must surely have had something after all. My Aunt Isa and Bella Smith were named after her.

The whole family was notable for a fervent evangelical piety, and they lived within reach of each other and in great amity. The two Smith families, Charles' and William's, were so large that they naturally divided themselves into the older lots and the younger lots, and my information is nearly all about the older set, my mother having been away from home before the later members of the family were born – she was 22 years older than Jessie.

Tom Smith, in Elgin, used to tell me about the outings they used to have once a year, over the hill to Midward and Montgarrie. They would leave home (his father William's farm) in the early morning and when they came to the top of the hill they would see the Midward children in the distance watching for the first sight of them. They all had dinner at Midward and called in at Montgarrie on their way home. Auntie of Montgarrie was a character, not always popular but quite inescapable, and the cousins never met in later life without exchanging anecdotes about her.

My grandfather Charles was, by all accounts, an outstanding personality. I never heard him mentioned without admiration: his own family, his nephews and nieces, and numerous neighbours all spoke of him in our hearing when we were children as having been 'by-ordinar'. My mother, in fact, worshipped him to such an extent that the worst thing she could say to any of us was 'What would your sainted grandfather have thought of you?' I well remember a terrible scene when my brother Charlie, who feared nobody, said 'I never saw the man. He doesn't matter to me.' If he had blasphemed the Almighty her reaction couldn't have been more violent, and I must admit that the rest of us were sufficiently shocked.

My mother's almost unnatural devotion to her father accounted probably for her antipathy to her mother. My grandparents had been an ideal couple, my grandmother sank her own personality in the Smith one, identified herself with all his church and evangelical interests and was an excellent wife and mother. My mother had a certain admiration for her looks; she had been very beautiful and even when I remember her as an old lady had looks that none of her six daughters inherited. Auntie Annie was pretty but insipid, my mother handsome, but all Smith, and the others quite ordinary and passable.

My grandfather was not a successful farmer, and they were quite poor – with ten children they could hardly have been anything else – but the other members of the family were well to do. Auntie of Montgarrie was, one gathers, a constantly recurring irritant in the home. The younger members of the family always spoke of her – they do still – with dislike but my mother seemed able to excuse anything to her because 'she was very dear to my father'.

Auntie Lizzie said to me lately when she was lying ill, 'I was remembering what Midward used to be like on a sunny summer morning. When my father went out, James Taylor at the next farm would shout "It's a fine morning, Charles" and my father would say, in his lovely voice, "Good morning, James"'.

I have been dipping into the life of William Robertson Smith which came this morning (1961). Many thanks for it. It's fascinating, so many familiar names, as familiar to me in my childhood as the names of film stars are to the youth of today – Begg, Rainy, Marcus Dods, White. Also Currie of Keig, with whose son and daughter we had a kind of a friendship in Glasgow. I see that WRS was the first child to be baptised in the Free Church of Keig. The book frequently gives me a lump in my throat, partly nostalgia, there's something so familiar about the atmosphere. Bits of it give me a real thrill but the behaviour of the Rainy, Moncrieff, Begg set-up is painful. Many people must have been ill-informed and adversely influenced about the WRS controversy. Ordinary people didn't have access to information as they have now and were at the mercy of their ministers for direction about such matters. What a tragic and

3

triumphant family the Smiths of Keig were. Scholarship on the WRS level was outwith the knowledge of neighbours of the Smith family. People who liked WRS were chiefly scholars on his own level. His opponents were more jealous than righteous. He wasn't physically attractive and that matters a lot to ordinary folk. I once heard my Aunt Lizzie say about my grandmother, 'Mother had no use for anybody who isn't bonnie and well-dressed'. Old Pirie Smith (WRS' father) looks delightful, his wife rather formidable. My mother spoke of them all as 'queer craiturs'. Her father was an elder at Keig before there was a Free Church in Alford. I have no recollection that my mother ever spoke of Pirie Smith visiting there, though Nicoll of Auchendoir did so frequently. The family at Midward, or at least part of it, knew Charles Murray, the poet. Uncle James was in school at the same time, if not in the same class. If you think they were proud of him, or admired him, you still don't know my relations. I used to be able to recite one or two of his poems. As to the Nicolls, Lumsden in winter would be as bleak as the Arctic regions, also as cut off from civilisation, especially before cycling and cars – in summer, glorious fresh air and space and freedom. One of the three granddaughters (Kirkcaldys) of William Robertson Nicoll was in your sister Isabel's class at the Aberdeen Girls' High School.

(Charles Murray doesn't belong to the family story. The Smiths of Keig and the Nicolls of Auchendoir do, not least on account of the Disruption of 1843 when – partly because of controversy over patronage, by which ministers could be imposed on congregations by patrons, many of them landowners – a large number of ministers and elders left the Church of Scotland to form the Free Church of Scotland. The landowner at Alford refused any site for a place of worship to the Free churchfolk there. They were forbidden the use, for worship, of various shops, then of a barn, then of a shed – which the landowner said should be used only for commercial purposes. So they held services on the highwayside. They tried setting up a tent – or 'clootie kirk' – then they settled in a barn over which the laird had no control. Parliamentary pressure eventually made proprietors withdraw refusal of sites. The Alford group was part of the Free Presbytery of Alford, and in the early days they were a branch of the Free congregation in the Keig and

Tough area, where the congregation had called William Pirie Smith, till then a headmaster in an Aberdeen school, to be their minister. They began in a wooden shed, then a stone church was built and at its inauguration Smith's eldest son, William Robertson Smith, was christened. WRS was to be one of the most controversial figures within the Free Church because he was to write for the *Encyclopaedia Britannica* suggesting that the Bible, though a revelation from God to man, was not sound as history. That Smith household, where the father continued to be a teacher, was a centre of intense intellectual activity, as was the other manse at that time in the Alford Free Presbytery where Harry Nicoll had, by going over to the Free Kirk, forfeited his position as a schoolmaster at Lumsden. The overruling power in Nicoll's life was the love of reading – the Midward family would later recall how he had gone with a wheelbarrow to wherever in the district there were books for sale. He amassed what was thought to be the largest library ever collected by a Scots minister. He was father of William Robertson Nicoll, who was to found the *British Weekly*, at one time a journal of great literary, religious and political influence. WRN was knighted and made a Companion of Honour.)

Charles Smith 'came out' at the Disruption in 1843 and was one of the elders who founded the Free Church of Alford to which he and his family walked four miles and back every Sunday. They didn't all go every Sunday for my mother had a story about being left in charge of the family when her parents went to church. She tried in vain to establish order amongst them and get them to work. Annie had got a smack which made her nose bleed. She promptly got a basin of water and let her nose bleed into it to impress her mother with the amount of blood she had lost.

Auntie of Montgarrie and her husband, always referred to in that order, also attended the Free Kirk: she always wore a grand silk dress on Sunday, unlike my grandmother who couldn't afford grandeur, and she ostentatiously carried a half-crown for the collection. It was a sore point with her that my grandmother, as wife of the leading elder and also a beautiful and gracious personality, took the place of the minister's wife at social functions, the then minister being a bachelor.

It has always been claimed for my grandmother that she bore

Auntie's impertinence with great patience because of their mutual devotion to Charles. Auntie Isa had a story about her mother getting material for a new dress – an unusual occurrence. She, Isa, was sent with it to Alford to be made up by the dressmaker. Montgarrie being half-way between Tullynessle and Alford, no member of the family would have dared to pass Auntie's door. The parcel had to be displayed and explained and Auntie said, 'Nonsense: it would cost too much to get it made at the dressmaker's. Leave it here and I'll make it.' The dress was botched and my poor grandmother got no pleasure out of it. I wish I could report that my grandfather dealt with his dear sister as she deserved but if he did I never heard of it.

There were cousins of my grandfather's who had some importance in the family story. There was a Mr Black who made a fortune in India as a tea merchant. He retired to Aberdeen and built Willowbank House, which is now the headquarters of the Health Welfare Service. When I was young, his son, a retired Indian Army General, and his sister, both unmarried, lived in Willowbank.

There were also Clerihews. One of them was a minister in Stirling, and his daughter was a missionary in Poona. I have a silver napkin ring which she sent me when she heard that I was getting married. My mother and she knew each other when they were young, but none of us ever saw her. Old Bella Clerihew who must have been an older member of the same Clerihew family lived in a cottage on Midward. My mother and her brothers Willie and James used to spend winter evenings in Bella Clerihew's house listening to hair-raising tales about ghosts and robbers. One of her stories was about a woman who opened a press door in her house, put in her hand in the dark and felt a man's head. So great was her presence of mind that she said; 'I forgot that I had left my brush there,' and closed and locked the door. This story scared them so terribly that when they went home Bella had to stand in her door till they reached safety. Every few minutes they would shout, 'Are you still there, Bella?' Bella also taught them the Robbers' Language (whereby a suffix, sometimes 'vers' was added to every word spoken, the sense then becoming available – it was thought – only to those in the know).

Another relative called Old Auntie lived for a time at Mid-

ward and died there in a little room off the kitchen. That must
have been after my mother left home because she never spoke of
her, and it was Auntie Isa who told me that the little room was a
place of terror for her. She had been taken to see the 'remains'
and afterwards used to be shut up in that room as a punishment.
That wasn't quite so cruel as it sounds because it was then and
much later quite customary to take children to view 'remains'
and it was considered an insult if grown-up people didn't visit a
house of mourning for that purpose.

The Midward menage seems to have been typical of the poor
but proud household of the times, bare living and high thinking
– especially in the religious sense. The younger members of the
family speak of the freedom of their life – the hills where they
gathered cranberries and the dam where they bathed. To my
mother the dam was just the place where she did the washing. As
the eldest of so large a family she had had more work and less
play than the others. She spoke of her mother as having had a
violent temper, so violent that it often brought on an attack of
bile. The chances are that it was because she was ill that she was
irritable. Moreover she must have been like the old woman who
lived in a shoe, though my mother claimed that she, Helen, bore
the burden of the large family because my grandmother always
devoted herself exclusively to the newest baby.

My grandmother's father, John Grant, was a land-steward,
and his father or grandfather had been a younger son of the Earl
of Seafield. His brother, Major Grant, was land steward at
Grantown and Nethybridge and was still remembered by the old
people at Nethy when your father and I went there. He was
never married. As a matter of interest in this connection – when
the young Earl of Seafield died my grandmother's brother,
Alexander Grant, considered that he was the heir. He had all
his papers in order but I don't know whether he ever put
forward his claim. For some reason which nobody could ever
explain to me, nobody succeeded to the title at this time. The
Earl's mother continued to be the Countess for many years. She
was still there, at Castle Grant in Grantown, when your father
went to Nethy. When she died the heir, father of the present
Countess, was some relation of hers – an Ogilvie and not a
Grant.

My grandmother's mother was called Helen Naughton or

Naughtie (pronounced Nachty). There is or was a well in Dufftown called Nellie Nachty's well. Helen Naughton's mother's name was Isabel More. We had a book at home *Duncan Matheson, the Scottish Evangelist* in which Isabel More is mentioned.

(I have failed to find the name of Isabel More in the book, but in the family she was reputed to be the person who figures in the account of Matheson arriving in 'a strange, out-of-the-way region, without a friend, without lodging and without means. It was drawing towards night and Matheson knew not where to go. Seeing a boy crossing a field, he called to him, and said, "Are there any godly people here about?" "Na, na", replied the lad, "there is nae sic fouk in this pairish." "Are there any believers?" asked the evangelist. "Bleevers," exclaimed the boy, "I never heerd o sic things." "Any religious people then?". "I dinnae ken ony o that kind; I doot they dinna come this road at a'". "Well then," said the missionary, making a last attempt, "are there any who keep family worship?" "Family worship?"'replied the lad "fat's that?" The boy, having taken his last stare at the curious stranger, was about to go. Matheson was at his wit's end when a happy thought struck him. "Stop," he cried, "are there any hypocrites hereabout?" "Ou, aye," replied the youth, brightening into intelligence, "the fouk say that ——'s wife is the greatest hypocrite in a' the pairish." "Where is her house ?" "Yonner by," said the lad, pointing to a house about a mile distant. Having rewarded his guide with a penny, the last he had, Matheson made his way to the dwelling of "the greatest hypocrite in the parish" and knocked at the door as the shades of night were falling. The door was opened by a tidy, cheerful, middle-aged matron, to whom the stranger thus addressed himself, "Will you receive a prophet in the name of a prophet, and you'll not lose your reward?" She smiled and bade him welcome. The hospitalities of that Christian home were heaped upon him and he spent a delightful evening in fellowship. In this way a lasting friendship began, and, what was better, a door of usefulness was opened to him'.)

There was always a certain amount of coming and going between the Grants and the Smiths, and we ourselves were on fairly intimate terms with Grants who lived in Elgin and were second cousins of ours. They are all now in Australia. My

8

mother remembered her parents going, when she was about six years old, to her Uncle James' wedding in Dufftown. A great many years later a bonnet was found in the loft at Mid Stocket Road after my grandmother died. None of my aunts had ever seen it before but my mother identified it as the one her mother had worn on that occasion.

My grandmother's loft was a family joke. It was reached by a ladder and nobody but herself was ever allowed into it. Evidently she spent hours in it when she got the house to herself. One afternoon the ladder slipped and she was a prisoner. She managed somehow to get up to the skylight and attract the attention of her next-door neighbour. When she died, it was found to be stocked with clothes – dresses and dolmans and bonnets some of which only my mother had ever seen before. She must have flitted them all from Alford to Aberdeen and to the three different houses she occupied in Aberdeen.

I think Auntie of Montgarrie was younger than my grandfather and was probably born about 1826. She was 84 about the time I was married – 1910. I have always understood that Dr Kidd baptised her (Dr James Kidd, 1761–1834, was Professor of Oriental Languages at Marischal College, Aberdeen, then minister, with a reputation for forceful preaching, at Gilcomston Church of Scotland Chapel-of-Ease). I don't know about her schooling except that she could read and write. My mother was at a Dame's School, so was her brother William. The younger members of the Midward family went to school in Alford. The headmaster of the school my uncles attended was a 'stickit' minister, that is a man who had trained for the ministry but failed to get a parish.

When Auntie of Montgarrie was quite young – 18 or so – she was married to Taylor Gardiner. I know nothing at all about him except that he died of smallpox and is buried in St Peter's Churchyard in Aberdeen. Auntie had then an infant a few months old and went home with him to her parents' house at Skene. This child died in childhood and she had no family to James Stewart whom she subsequently married. Incidentally my grandfather was said to have had small-pox when he was born. At any rate his mother had it. Auntie was small and dark and her chief characteristic was an inordinate distress over other people's sins and shortcomings. Her husband's nephew was apprenticed with him as a blacksmith and lived with them. Auntie found him a great burden on her spirit because he wasn't TT. She used to go ben to the 'room' when he was at his dinner, after they had finished theirs, and sing for his edification, 'Have courage, my boy, to say NO'. She used to say that her knees were like brass with praying for him. Jimmie Donald was his name and I remember going with Auntie to visit him when he was a middle-aged man with a grown-up family and being surprised to find that he was an eminently respectable citizen with a smart wife and good-looking children.

My Aunt Annie was named after Auntie of Montgarrie and was a favourite, 'Annie is like me temporally and spiritually' Auntie would say, quite mistakenly.

Her neighbours, the Macdonalds, were the first people in the neighbourhood to play croquet. She had heard that they had a lawn laid out for the purpose and was shocked to hear of their frivolity. In order to see for herself how depraved they were, she went one afternoon, when she knew they were having a party, on to the roof of her henhouse, but it was in a poor condition and collapsed and poor Auntie fell in amongst the hens. In spite of the croquet, however, she respected young Willie Macdonald sufficiently to vote for him when there was an election of elders. The minister asked her if she had made up her mind about her vote and she said, 'I'm going to vote for a man who can both sing and pray.' The Macdonalds had a wool mill in Montgarrie. Up to the time I was married we wore costumes and suits of Montgarrie tweed. There was a sizeable Macdonald family, several of whom I remember. One of them, Murdo, was a divinity student, lodging in Rosemount Place at Mile End. He was one of the highly gifted young men who didn't finish his studies. He died in the mental hospital about 60 years ago. Willie was the youngest of the family.

Auntie of Montgarrie must have been a great trial to her minister. If the sermon wasn't pleasing her she took her Bible in her hand and turned over the leaves, and said on the way out of church that the sermon was 'just tooter'. Once, when she heard that the minister was going to take the chair at a concert, she was very angry and told him so. 'But Mrs Stewart,' he said, 'St Paul says that all things are lawful.' 'Ay', she said, 'but finish the text. He says All things are not expedient.'

Bare Living, High Thinking

I remember going to a C of E service when my sister Jessie and I were at Montgarrie for a weekend. The Laird of Whitehaugh – I can't remember his name, maybe it was double-barrelled – was not resident but was a C of E minister and when he came on holiday he conducted services in the small chapel on the estate. Auntie had a great personal regard for him because he was a good man and because he had an unhappy background. One gathers that he also thought highly of her and visited her often. The story about his background is that his great-great-etc-grandfather was cursed by a gipsy woman because he set his dogs on her boy. I don't know to what extent the boy was damaged. It did happen that the man and all his successors died in accidents. The laird who became a minister and whose appearance I remember clearly never married. I hate to say it but he committed suicide.

My mother always said that Auntie was very kind to them when they were children but the younger ones have a different story. Some years ago, your sister Helen took the Mid Stocket Aunts and myself out to Tullynessle Churchyard. We passed a cottage which Isa pointed out as having been the abode of a woman who used to take them in on their way to school and give them a piece and jam. 'So different from Auntie,' Isa said. 'If she gave us anything it was a dry crust.' They took lunch with them when they left home but always ate it all before they reached school three miles away.

Uncle John was apprenticed as a youth to a carpenter in Keig. It must have been a biggish concern because the apprentices all lived in a bothy and went home at the weekends. John called at Auntie's on his way home and one weekend she invited him to have his tea with her on his way back. Accordingly when he left home the following day he went without his tea, but Auntie had changed her mind and said, 'Your mother would never have let you away without your tea' and didn't give him anything. He had another four miles to walk to Keig. She used, however, to write him kind letters when he was away. Her writing had to be seen to be believed. When one of her letters arrived in Aberdeen (within my recollection) it was passed round all the relations to be deciphered. Her spelling, too, was individual. She spelt 'how' 'hogh'. Uncle John once mislaid one of her letters and it was found by another of the apprentices and read and spelt aloud to the occupants of the bothy. It was addressed 'My dear nephew'. Nobody claimed it, and nobody laughed louder than Uncle John, but when the reader laid it down John said, 'She seems to be a nice wifie.'

My mother used to tell how her father died at the age of 59. When my grandmother bent over him he was heard to say:

> I've loved Thee in life, I'll love Thee in death,
> I'll praise Thee as long as Thou lendest me breath
> And sing when the death dew lies cold on my brow
> If ever I loved Thee, my Jesus, 'tis now.

When he died there were still four of the children under fourteen years of age. It is still a sore point with my aunts that Auntie wouldn't allow my grandmother to give tea to the relatives who came from a distance to the funeral. At my mother's marriage shortly afterwards Auntie decreed that the four youngest sisters were not to have dinner with the company, but though they were disappointed at the time they had an excellent dinner off the leavings. The marriage was a great occasion for them and Isa spent all her money, 1s10d, on a carafe and tumbler, which we still have in this house. Isa went to Alford to buy it and sat down at the roadside several times on the way home to take it out of its paper and admire it.

After my grandfather's death the farm was carried on by my Uncle Willie who was the oldest son. He was quite young, had no experience other than what he had got at home and had half a dozen younger brothers and sisters dependent on him. Moreover, there was no money. By this time my mother, James and Annie were away, Charlie and John were apprenticed joiners and the four young girls at school. Charlie was only 14 months older than John; my mother attributed his many peculiarities to that fact, asserting that he resented being ousted from the cradle. Whatever the reason, he was a strange dour character. When he went home at the weekends in the winter his mother and Isa used to put on shawls and go to meet him in case he was lonely on the dark roads but he wouldn't even bother to acknowledge their presence. Willie was very different. His sisters always went to meet him when he came home from the market and he said, 'Hullo dearies' and gave them plunky (a sweet made of flour and treacle or syrup. The mixture was boiled, then plunged into cold water to make it harden. In the 1930s large quantities of it were sold in the New Market in Market Street, Aberdeen).

James started his career as a clerk in the station at White-house, then at the Railway Station in Aberdeen. He was later secretary to Mr Byres, the laird of Tonleigh, and then assistant evangelist in the Gordon Mission. He had considerable gifts as a preacher and was well known as an evangelist in the North-east counties and in Orkney and Shetland. Uncle John some years later also joined the Gordon Mission. James became Super-intendent in course of time, and when he died John succeeded him. This departure accounts, I think, for the Separatist ten-dency in the whole family. My grandmother was a staunch churchwoman and never cared much about the Mission, but whilst all their Auchmar cousins were elders in their respective churches, the Midward family ultimately joined either the Gordon Mission, the Plymouth Brethren or the Baptists. Even my mother was a Baptist till her marriage. James was the dominant member of the family and kept all the other members of it under his heel. My mother thought him wonderful for a long time, and even when she had to acknowledge his faults still stood in awe of him. She once admitted to me that in his early days as a preacher he was somewhat above himself and when she said something was awful he said, 'Don't use that word. There's nothing awful but the wrath of God.'

The farm, never very prosperous, came to grief altogether under Willie's management. There are two distinct reports about the reasons for that. One is that he was extravagant, knew very little about farming, rode about on a horse (though there was no other transport and they were four miles from the nearest village), was too much interested in singing and was something of a ladies' man. Also he had borrowed £70 from Auntie of Montgarrie. The other is that though he was a beautiful singer, having inherited his father's lovely voice, and was for several years precentor in Alford Church, he got no salary. The farm had never been prosper-ous, he had to provide for all the younger members of the family and there was every prospect that things would get steadily worse for years. As for the £70 he owed Auntie, he had done all the work of their small croft and garden for years entirely free of charge, but the £70 debt more or less dogged his footsteps all his life.

The farm was sold up and the whole family moved into a house in Torry, and my father and mother into one in Rosemount Place. It wasn't a particularly happy home at Torry. The sons were all unmarried, James was obviously in command, Willie unhappy and slighted, Charlie dour and resentful and given to making cutting remarks to Willie, John good-humoured but negligible. Willie soon married and got out of it. He married Jeannie Gordon, from Alford, became a commercial traveller and settled at Kittybrewster. From this time on James was looked on as the head of the family. He was said to have paid the £70 to Auntie, though goodness knows where he got the money, and thus saved them from disgrace. My grandmother must have had a pretty poor time. She was absolutely penniless and dependent for the rest of her life on what her family chose to give her. To be sure, they provided well for her, each of her sons contributed a weekly sum. My father gave her and Auntie of Montgarrie all their footwear free of charge from the day of his marriage till he gave up business 25 years later. Her daughters lived with her and paid the household expenses.

Lizzie who at ten was considered too old for school when they left Alford and too young to go out to work, stayed for a year or more with my parents and daily took my sister Jessie out in the pram. She says they were extremely kind to her and gave her the first really nice dress she ever had. Charlie was a frequent visitor, my mother being the only one of the family he liked or who liked him. She made cocoa for him and he sent Lizzie to Ledinghams for a bag of broken biscuits. Sometimes he gave the baby a bit of biscuit but never shared them with anybody else.

Bare Living, High Thinking

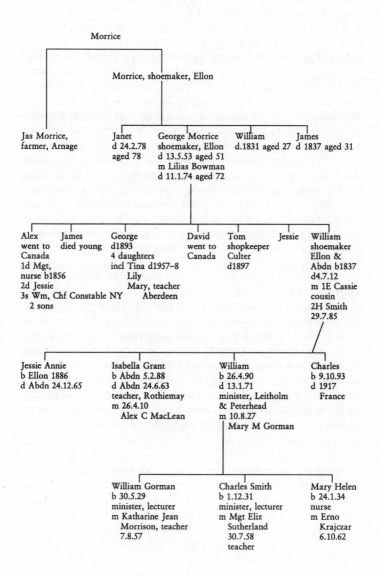

Morrice

Morrice, shoemaker, Ellon

Jas Morrice,
farmer, Arnage

Janet
d 24.2.78
aged 78

George Morrice
shoemaker, Ellon
d 13.5.53 aged 51
m Lilias Bowman
d 11.1.74 aged 72

William
d.1831 aged 27

James
d 1837 aged 31

Alex
went to
Canada
1d Mgt,
nurse b1856
2d Jessie
3s Wm, Chf Constable NY
2 sons

James
died young

George
d1893
4 daughters
incl Tina d1957–8
Lily
Mary, teacher
Aberdeen

David
went to
Canada

Tom
shopkeeper
Culter
d1897

Jessie

William
shoemaker
Ellon &
Abdn b1837
d4.7.12
m 1E Cassie
cousin
2H Smith
29.7.85

Jessie Annie
b Ellon 1886
d Abdn 24.12.65

Isabella Grant
b Abdn 5.2.88
d Abdn 24.6.63
teacher, Rothiemay
m 26.4.10
Alex C MacLean

William
b 26.4.90
d 13.1.71
minister, Leitholm
& Peterhead
m 10.8.27
Mary M Gorman

Charles
b 9.10.93
d 1917
France

William Gorman
b 30.5.29
minister, lecturer
m Katharine Jean
Morrison, teacher
7.8.57

Charles Smith
b 1.12.31
minister, lecturer
m Mgt Eliz
Sutherland
30.7.58
teacher

Mary Helen
b 24.1.34
nurse
m Erno
Krajczar
6.10.62

15

2

A DIFFERENCE IN TEMPERAMENT

My mother was the victim of a peculiar background, a father whom she idolised and a mother she disliked. The affection she had for her father she transferred to her brother James – JA as he was subsequently called. She and JA were together in Aberdeen isolated from the rest of the family when they were fairly young – JA a clerk at the Railway Station and my mother with Mr and Mrs Collie as general factotum and family friend. The only son of the house, a student in her time with them, was English Presbyterian minister in Birkenhead, and as long as he lived he never came to Aberdeen without spending an afternoon in our house. I remember him well.My mother had been very good to JA and the Collies allowed her to have him a lot about the house and she used to say that they had always meant a lot to each other. She did think he was the world's wonder. She was sadly disillusioned, poor soul, but not till much later.

My mother and her sister Annie were then six years together in London. My mother's health broke down and she went home to Alford but Annie remained in London. I don't know what ailed my mother but she was neither welcome nor happy at home. She must have gone home almost immediately after her father's death, perhaps because of it. My grandmother must have been in a sad way, my grandfather having recently died, no money. Uncle Willie, a mere lad, making no success of farming and a household of three boys and four girls still in the place. There was no sympathy between my mother and hers, and when a mutual friend, James Simpson, a native of Alford but living in Ellon, suggested that she might go to keep house for my father, she went. My sister Jessie said that my mother once said to her that, after being at home, living with my father was incredible peace. My parents were married in July 1885. My sister Jessie was born in June 1886.

My father had a shoemaker's business in Ellon, and his father and grandfather had it before him. His father, George Morrice, apprenticed all his six sons, Alex, James, George, David, Tom and William to his own trade but my father was the only one who remained in it. His mother, Lillias Bowman, also belonged to Ellon. Her photograph shows her to have been a rather grim, heavy-featured woman and my father said very little about her except that she was a fine singer and could learn a new tune after she was 70.

My grandfather, like the Smith one, came out at the Disruption and my father's earliest recollections – he was born in 1837 – were connected with that event. He remembered seeing the evangelist Robert Murray McCheyne (1813–43) pelted with eggs in the Market Square in Ellon when he was preaching there, and my grandmother, who wasn't sympathetic about the Disruption, saying to his father as he was leaving for a service on a Sunday morning, 'You'd better take your Free Kirk brats with you'. She afterwards accompanied him to the Free Church but all her relatives remained in the Auld Kirk.

The book *Short Stories by the author of Johnny Gibb of Gushetneuk* gives a grim picture of life in Northeast Scotland. The odd thing is that it drew my attention to something I hadn't noticed before. The background is exactly my father's – Buchan etc – but it had never before occurred to me that my father never complained of having known poverty in his youth – obviously he hadn't. There were no stories of privations, real or imagined, very different to my mother whose background was largely pathos. I fancy that my Morrice grandfather and his sons had a very flourishing business. There is, too, a difference in temperament to reckon with. Things didn't matter to my father – ideas did. To my mother anything that didn't please her was a personal affront.

My father had been previously married to a cousin of his own, Elizabeth Cassie, but I think she died in a year or so. Her photograph was in our Family Album but my mother was very touchy about it and I never heard my father refer to her. I can't imagine what my mother would have thought if she had known that I once confided to my boon companion, Alice Davidson, that my father had had another wife and I even suggested quite untruthfully that I had a grown-up half-brother somewhere abroad.

I know very little about the two years my mother spent in Ellon. Jessie Annie was born there and was named after my father's only sister, Jessie, and my mother's sister, Annie, and to save ill-feeling was called by both names. It was a grievance to my mother and my grandmother that she wasn't called by the latter's name – Isabella.

My father's sister had been an invalid for 17 years 'in a decline', though Mrs George Morrice vowed that she was only neurotic. In any case, my father was devoted to her, had attended to her for years and thought her very clever. Our house was full of fine needlework and lace and there was a handsome crochet bedcover which should have been preserved as an heirloom. It was all her work.

I have never understood why my father gave up a good long-established business to take his chance amongst strangers in Aberdeen. He had stood security for his brother George who had a bookseller's business in Broad Street. George failed and brought my father down with him. My mother never liked Ellon and the disaster may have provided a pretext, especially as the Midward family was also removing to Aberdeen.

Lizzie says that my mother at this time was very discontented, that she complained constantly of her fallen fortunes and blamed George Morrice and his wife for them. Perhaps the state of her mind at that time accounts for the fact that she was very hard on Jessie A and used to smack her when she was the merest infant. I know that later she blamed herself bitterly for that. My father was infinitely patient and good-tempered. He always cited his brother George as having been the very pattern of laziness. George never did anything but read, though he seems to have read to some purpose. I had a teacher in the Central School who said she owed him a great deal. She went to his shop as a message girl and when he discovered that she would like to be a teacher he taught her himself and saw her through all her exams till she got into college. His wife took a poor view of this, but she was a clever, domineering woman and took the business into her own hands.

By the time I was born, when Jessie A was 18 months old, fortunes had begun to mend a little all round. I was named after my grandmother and was always for that reason her favourite grandchild. My Uncle Charlie went away to Edinburgh, Annie

A Difference in Temperament

to London, Mary to Edinburgh, and Isa to learn nursing. Lizzie went home and started work in the office of the drapery business of George Bowman who was my father's cousin.

We removed to Thomson Street and my grandmother and Lizzie and Jessie to Lilybank Place. James and John were seldom at home because they were on the staff, at that time considerable, of the Gordon Mission and were away conducting missions. We had a carefree, happy time in Thomson Street, the Victoria Park was at our door and we played in it all the time. There were plenty of children of our own age, no traffic worth mentioning on the street and none to make us afraid. I often feel much nearer to the days when I played in the Victoria Park than when I lived in Harcourt Road in the 1930s.

I have never cultivated the anniversary memory. My mother was a solemn warning. She was forever saying 'So and so died so many years ago today' and she could weep as bitterly every time. She regulated her whole life, and ours, by the expectation that my father, being 20 years older than herself, would die and leave her penniless. He lived to see even the youngest old enough to work for his living. But that fear of my mother's regulated our whole life. We had to ignore the impertinence of our relatives in case we might some day be poor enough to need their help. Several years before my father died, probably when he was 70 – he was 76 when he died – Jessie A and I were due to get new costumes. They were made by a dressmaker and the material was got from the Montgarrie Mills. They were black, and when my father saw them he was thoroughly annoyed and said to her, 'You might have waited for their mourning till they needed them'.

I have never liked Hogmanay or New Year's Day. Somehow Christmas Day escaped my mother's anniversary doldrums but the New Year didn't and there used to be such tearful and fearful forebodings that I gladly go early to bed on Hogmanay and leave everybody else to it.

I doubt whether my mother ever attended a concert in her life. She got a great thrill once at a church social meeting when she was a young girl. The minister read and recited 'If you're waking call me early, call me early mother dear'. It suited her over-emotional temperament and she never forgot it. She confided in her aunt, Mrs John Smith, that she would love to have it and

learn it, and her aunt said she was sure the minister would lend
her the book, but to borrow a book from the minister would
have been very bold behaviour.

My father in his younger days had gone to dances and
theatres, but that was a dark past he was discouraged from
mentioning. He had been what my mother would have called
godless in his youth. To mention those dark matters before his
family was bad, but to have done so before the Smith relations
would have been an irretrievable disaster. My father could touch
off any situation with a quotation from Burns – to my mother's
undisguised contempt. To her, Robbie Burns was a dissolute
profligate and a drunkard, nothing else. But my father couldn't
refrain sometimes from singing 'Hey Johnny Cope are you
waukin yet?' and taking a few dance steps when he had Charlie
in his arms, and she would say warningly, 'Now William!'.

The fact is that music meant nothing to her. She couldn't
recognise a tune, much less sing one. My grandmother was never
known to sing even to one of her babies but my mother did sing
in church, and was a great trial to us. It was impossible to keep
to a tune in her vicinity. Songs were outside her ken altogether
and hymns meant only words. She once said 'What's Annie
Laurie to me?' Only one here and there of the connections was
musical – Uncle Willie and his daughter Winnie, Uncle Charlie's
son Jack and my brother Charlie. Winnie and Jack, so far as I
know, enjoyed complete freedom but Charlie was never out of
trouble for his worldliness.

My father's friends foregathered in the back shop. If there was
an election or any other political excitement, my uncles James
and John, who took little enough notice at other times, called in
to discuss the situation with him. He was an ardent Liberal and
it was his proud boast that he had been present at the great
Liberal rally at Haddo House in 1884 when Mr Gladstone,
standing on the balcony, addressed 3,000 people and every word
was heard at the farthest edge of the crowd. But my father's
visitors were mostly his own relations or old acquaintances from
Ellon. He had a number of cousins, Wills, Bowmans and
Cassies, but they were too old to be of interest to us, and my
mother didn't care for them, though they were nice men and
prosperous. They were Auld Kirkers and not given to talking
about revivals and evangelistic meetings. My mother didn't care

A Difference in Temperament

for Mrs George Morrice and her four daughters though they were neighbours and went to the same church.

The question of Christian giving was discussed *ad nauseam* in our house when we were young and I still don't know who was right. My father said that if he gave us children a halfpenny four times every Sunday he was giving more than most, considering his circumstances. There were, of course, all the other collections, and a halfpenny was not negligible at that time. My mother said we shouldn't be brought up to give the smallest coin. Mr McGilp, a bachelor, once preached a sermon in which he said a minimum of one tenth should be given. A lot of people protested that if people had family obligations that was impossible.

Unfortunately my father was a very poor businessman. He used leather that was too expensive for mending purposes, he made boots for people with deformed feet, was in fact the only shoemaker in Aberdeen who could do it, but didn't charge enough to pay him for the time he spent on them. He lacked the ruthlessness to make people pay their accounts, and altogether he couldn't and didn't make money. He often declared, 'God sees the soles as well as the uppers'.

I can't remember having had any feeling of irritation or annoyance at my father, but many a night wallowed in thoughts of how bitterly my mother would weep at my funeral when she thought of how unjust she had been to so perfect a daughter. Not that she had any particular spite at me, I was pretty well able to keep off myself, but she was quite unreasonable. The perfect neighbour, the faithful friend, the charming hostess – she was all of these – but it was never possible to return to the house and be sure that fury wasn't waiting. That was for the four children, my father might get peevishness and complaints but not rows. Quiet though he was she wouldn't have dared. She was by no means constantly, perhaps not very often, in a temper, but there was no security. A dish was never broken by accident, always out of genuine, considered malice. She thought nothing of saying 'I hate the sight of you' or 'I wish you had never been born' and though she would say she was sorry she had lost her temper she would never admit that she had said these things. In spite of all that, she was very patient with anybody who was ill and gave them every possible attention.

Your father found her most entertaining. Her expressive face and emotional utterances were a constant joy to him. I found them irritating and embarrassing. I was sitting with my mother one day at an upstairs window in Leitholm Manse when a funeral came down to Coldstream Road. Evidently she knew all the circumstances – it was a child's funeral – and she said, tearfully, of the mother, 'Well she's had her last sight of the little box . . .' I thought I would never forgive her. How could she put that into words?

Well, in spite of all that she was an interesting personality. She had considerable intuitive cleverness – mother wit, whatever you like to call it – and a fantastic memory, but no logic and very little skill with her hands. Above all things she admired eloquence. My father was like Moses, slow of speech. He went to the prayer meeting with her every week, Wednesday being his half-holiday, but if he had 'led in prayer' her cup of bliss would be full. 'Gifted in prayer' was one of the expressions she used.

She was easily amused, pathetically grateful for any little present or attention but had no real sense of humour and was easily offended. When she died my brother Willie got a letter – there were scores of them – from an old minister who had spent a weekend taking services for him. The old minister thought she was a wonderful woman and put the matter in a nutshell when he said 'Her trumpet had no uncertain sound'. Nothing and nobody could have diverted my mother from what she thought right, and she had a great feeling for 'the fitness of things'. She was also an ardent churchwoman – evangelical but not standing for any nonsense about laymen aping the clergy. She was uncertain tempered, hysterical and difficult to live with, but there was no question whatsoever about unworthy ideals. She was quite incapable of telling a lie, or of acting with meanness or self-interest.

Many of my stories about my mother give a wrong impression of her whereas I can't think of any incident about my father which wouldn't fit in with the general impression of quiet integrity, kindly humour and unfailing patience.

The Mid Stocket folk (Aunts Isa, Lizzie and Jessie) gave a text box to my mother (this was a box full of texts tightly wrapped individually: the box was offered to guests or handed round a family and each would extract a text). The only time I recall it being used was when my brother Willie was going to an exam. My mother handed it to him, he reluctantly took one and it said, 'Whom the Lord loveth he chastiseth'. She said 'That won't do, take another' and she was never allowed to forget it. My mother used to speak with a kind of tearful elation about being 'caught up to meet Him in the air' – a prospect that always filled me with horror – *re* the idea of the Second Coming.

I was impressed with the idea of William Robertson Smith that so many of his friends had, that his knowledge as compared with others was less a matter of degree than of kind. It describes, to take a humble example, the difference between my parents. My mother had a wonderful memory, was quick-witted and could express herself freely but she lacked a kind of fundamental understanding. My father read very slowly and carefully and made no remarks about what he read unless he was questioned. If I wanted a thing explained I went to my father. He had an amazing flair for mathematics. His schooling had been almost non-existent but when we were learning Higher Mathematics he would work out complicated problems in arithmetic and algebra by methods of his own. He was a great admirer of Hugh Miller, had read everything he ever wrote and remembered it. He was interested in astronomy too and had theories about the possibility of people learning to fly. My mother was a voracious reader of history, romance and sermons, and had a phenomenal memory, but a scientific fact was of no interest to her. Like William Robertson Nicoll she would have hated to see the inside of a watch.

My mother read a great deal but not widely: stories and sermons and religious books, but her standards were not literary – romantic and religious rather. *Adam Bede* she would approve – moral problems were involved. As for plays, I'm quite sure she never saw one. My father had gone to plays and dances in his younger days but that was in a dark past never spoken of in the family. You must remember that her attitude was fairly common – Howard Spring says that a lifetime of going to the theatre didn't cure him of a feeling that it was a wonder disaster didn't overtake him for going. My father's reading was of a different kind but he was much better educated than my mother. Her attitude to education was, I think, fairly normal – the desire to make the best of such talents as are obvious. She wasn't money-minded nor particularly utilitarian and if there was some feeling of being upsides with her relatives it wasn't too surprising. George MacDonald says, 'The inconsistent never can be understood'. My mother was morally consistent. She would have gone jocund to the stake. Intellectually she was all at sea, no logic in her at all.

George MacDonald was in general thought to have been unorthodox but the people who thought that seemed to enjoy his novels. My father didn't let other people's beliefs worry him unduly but my mother had a way of attaching labels to them – 'He is a perfectionist' or 'He believes in the Larger Hope'.

I have heard my mother say that every time a child was born to her she said, 'Another soul to train for eternity'. I always had great difficulty in believing it and certainly was never within reach of feeling it. What a mercy my father was a quiet man. She certainly was an outsize character. Your father found her endlessly diverting – a Dickensian character. She was the only person I ever knew who could and did toss her head. She might have made a tragedy actress. She could say things without a tremor that I couldn't think of without bursting into tears. After I was married and paid her visits she would often bid me farewell with a verse of Scripture or a few lines of a hymn, with the result that I set off for home with shattered nerves, not sure whether to succumb to the misery of the situation or to be furious with her for creating it.

The Free Church General Assembly of 1878 (at which William Robertson Smith was removed from his professorial chair at the Free Church College in Aberdeen because of the views he expressed in *Encyclopaedia Britannica* articles about the historical authenticity of parts of the Bible) was an old story before we were taking notice, but the name of Robertson Smith was very familiar to us. The Higher Critics were to Uncle James and his kind something akin to the Kaiser and Hitler to later generations. My mother was something between him and my father. She looked upon learning with favour and without what seems to have been the bitter jealousy with which Uncle James regarded it. My father's attitude lacked the hyper-evangelical fervour and accepted facts without personal bias. 'Facts are chiels that winnae ding' was a favourite saying with him.

My father had a great repertoire of funny stories, quotations from Burns, and verses of Scripture, which he used with considerable effect, but he rarely obtruded his opinions, and when he did it was very haltingly. He had a bad stammer as a boy and he said his brothers made fun of him, so he learnt to be silent. All the same, he hadn't a natural gift of speech. My mother's folk treated him so shabbily that I was very grateful to your father who genuinely admired him and valued his opinions. Dr Christie, a cynical ill-tempered man, said to my mother once when she was showing him out, 'What a dear old man that is.'

I am not sorry that I was brought up by two people so differently constituted as my father and mother. It has perhaps given me some appreciation of how utterly different two people can be and still be sincere practising Christians. My father's mind was so reasoning and well-balanced and independent that I never cease to wonder at it.

3

SUSTAINED BY RIGHTEOUSNESS

One of my early recollections is of going out to the street in the morning and meeting Alick Morgan who was two or three years older. He said, 'Well, the war will be begun by now' and proceeded to give me a lurid account of what a war was like; my heart sickened with horror. That must have been the Spanish-American War in the Philippines (1894).

The earliest record of my intimidating personality goes further back than that. Before my brother Willie was born my mother had been taking a rest in the afternoon whilst Jessie A, and I (three and a half and two respectively) were playing on the rug at the fire. We had been making too much noise and she got up and smacked us. I was, justly, annoyed and said to Jessie A 'We won't stand any of her nonsense, will we?' I don't of course remember that but I do remember that once before we were at school Jessie A and I were playing in our bedroom. We had, as the fashion was, long hair and my mother was very proud of it. I pleated JA's hair and told her that it was a lovely pleat; she said she wished she could see it. So I promptly cut it off and showed it to her, whereupon she seized the scissors and cut off handfuls of my hair. Our screams at the sight of our hair in a heap on the floor brought my mother. Perhaps it's as well that I have no recollection of what happened then. Jessie A got her hair cut short like a boy's; mine, not having been cut to the bone, was just trimmed, mercifully, because my head, having a big lump on the back was considered an ugly shape.

Willie had infantile paralysis – polio – when he was a year old and needed a great deal of nursing, which he certainly got. My mother was at her very best when we were ill and grudged us nothing. When Willie did at length begin to walk his legs were very bent, but his speech was even more affected: he couldn't speak at all intelligibly till he was about seven. My father made boots for him of his own design, with hinged knees, and there were flat iron strips at the outer sides of the legs. I can remember that my mother used to cry when she was buckling on the boots. His legs straightened up quite soon but not before some of my relatives had made life intolerable to my mother by referring to him as if he were an imbecile. One day she went, as she very seldom did, to visit her mother at Lilybank Road. My grandmother could be very tactless, especially to her, and told her that she had had a painter working in the house, he had very bowed legs and she had said to 'the lassies' (Lizzie and Jessie), 'It's just a job like that that poor Willie Morrice will be fit for'.

Charlie Smith was a year older than Willie and constantly being referred to as being so pretty and clever – not by his parents Uncle Willie and Auntie Jeannie. They were in all circumstances understanding and kind. It was hardly to be wondered at that when the cousins eventually went to the same school and Willie first overtook Charlie Smith and then was a year ahead of him, though he never could get marks for reading, my mother felt that she had won a victory. But that is anticipating.

I was five and a half when my brother Charlie was born. He was a remarkably beautiful child and never outgrew his good looks. Uncle James had already been married for a year before Charlie was born. Agnes Measures, Uncle James' wife, was English and there was no celebration in Aberdeen.

Uncle Charlie married Margaret Ingram about this time and I was at the wedding. My parents were invited but Mother couldn't go and Jessie A was to go in her place. She however took earache and I accompanied my father. It was a great occasion for me. The wedding took place at the Ingrams' house. I have no recollection of the lunch but Auntie Maggie's nephews and nieces, the Macphersons, and I played all afternoon in the garden and made frequent journeys to the dining room to eat cakes and drink lemonade out of siphons. Moreover I was dressed in pale blue and was much admired and complimented – by the Ingrams, not the Smiths, compliments not being part of their habitual language.

When I got home I innocently dealt a severe blow to my mother's pride. I remarked that my father had helped to entertain the company by singing 'Annie Laurie'. He had a good tenor voice and sang well and was quite knowledgeable about music, but songs were taboo in the whole family connection. To say that she was annoyed would be quite inadequate – she was mortified. I doubt whether she dared say anything to him about it but she often referred to it afterwards when listing her grievances.

I remember being taken when I was five or six to see my Uncle George who for some years before his death lived next door to us. My father lifted me up to look at Uncle George in his coffin and I can still see the pained look on my father's face when I laughed aloud. I was also at Uncle George's funeral, and with my cousins who were all older than me looked through the Venetian blinds to see the funeral leaving the door. After it had left, my cousins and I, and a relative of their mother's who must have been a fool, sat down to a meal. It was a hilarious occasion and I remember the woman saying that I was a 'wee dumpling'. And that reminds me of another story. One day as I was coming home from school I met Mr Cable who was a kind of unofficial uncle of ours. He was on his way to a funeral, and I went home and told my mother that I had met Mr Cable and he had on a coffin hat and a communion jacket.

There was no ill-feeling between our household and the (George) Morrices. They frequented the house at all times, and one summer when they went to Lumphanan for a month's holiday they took me with them for the first fortnight and Jessie A for the second, and were extremely kind. Lily and I went every day along the railway line to a farm to get the milk. An Aberdeen family was lodging there and two of the girls waylaid us several times and took us into the house to admire an old Family Bible they had discovered. The ostensible reason was to show us that the *ss* were all written like *fs*. What they really did was to show us all the less genteel portions of Scripture. *Adam Bede* was a serial in the *Christian Herald* at the time, so the Poysers always attended the church on the hill at Lumphanan, and in the garden of the house where we stayed Adam Bede walks with Hetty Sorrel.

It was when Charlie was a baby that we had our first and last holiday as a family. It seems to me that it lasted all the summer but was probably only a month. We went to Skene, drove the few miles in the milkman's cart and stayed in the cottage of a Mrs Thomson. My father walked out on the Saturday evenings and went back on the Sundays. I remember getting a bantam's egg from Mrs Thomson and having kept it in my pocket for several days to show to him. I broke it just before he arrived. There were box beds in the two downstairs rooms and a square garden in front with a low drystane dyke round it. That garden, for me, was always the place where Ali Baba and his forty thieves hid their casks. We had a wonderful time, went to a farm every day for the milk and played with the children there. And there was a waste space near the house where caraway seeds grew.

As soon as I was old enough to find my own way from Thomson Street to Lilybank Place I went to see my grandmother every Saturday forenoon and continued to do so till I was practically grown up. To avoid meeting droves of cattle on their way to the Auction Mart I often went down Hutcheon Street and up George Street rather than by Berryden Road. She was usually alone when I arrived, so we exchanged news and drank tea together and then I watched her baking oatcakes on the girdle and browning milk puddings in a Dutch oven in front of the fire. It is positively true that I didn't feel any difference in age between us. My aunts Lizzie and Jessie who were at this time what is now called teenagers came to see us on Saturday evenings. We counted on their visit and were thoroughly aggrieved if they didn't turn up.

Old Uncle James Stewart died at Montgarrie when my brother Charlie was about four years old, at any rate before he had gone to school. Auntie sent in a wooden box full of quite useless clothes and a bundle of white linen collars, the kind that stood straight up and had turned-back points in front. Charlie was in bed with whooping-cough, not very ill, and the sight of the collars so inspired him that every day he sat up in bed with a collar on and preached. 'Ma,' said he one day, 'is Queen Victoria a good woman?'. 'Oh yes.' 'Is she the best woman in the world?' 'Maybe.' 'Ah!' solemnly shaking his head, 'but I know a better – Mary, God's wife.' 'Oh Charlie,' said my mother 'Mary isn't God's wife.' 'She must be,' he said, 'She's Jesus' mother and God is Jesus' father.'

He was well accustomed with preaching by this time. We were all taken to church at a very early age, and except for Charlie behaved excellently. The first day he was in church he tickled the back of a man's neck and the bald head of another. I haven't much patience with talk about children being forced to go to church and hating it for ever thereafter. We never thought of not going to church and we loved the Sunday School. Going to church was a family affair, we all went, and all our chums went to Sunday School. We were expected to remember the text and to be able to tell what the Sunday School lesson was about. It was an excellent training in concentration.

Moreover there was the pleasure of seeing all our friends and acquaintances in their Sunday best. We not only had a special dress for Sunday but our underclothes, shoes, stockings and hat were all sacred to Sunday. On one occasion only was the Sunday dress worn on a week-day and that was at the yearly school examination. 'Be sure you have on your Sunday dresses,' the teacher said. There was also a Bible examination but for that we only got a new pinafore. Some children we knew of put pinafores over their Sunday dresses when they sat down to dinner, but that was slovenly and lazy, and in our house the dress had to be changed and then changed again for Sunday School. It was a wonderful thought that next year this grandeur would be worn to school.

Our dresses were made by Miss Morrison, a dressmaker who lived in Loanhead Place. I still take an occasional look at the window of the room where we got them tried on. She made our clothes and my mother's for so many years that she was an intimate friend of the family. A Miss Laird in Dee Street trimmed our hats. My mother scarcely ever went out except to church and prayer meeting, and at an incredibly early age Jessie and I did all the errands. My mother would put her bonnet in a tin band-box and say, 'Tell Miss Laird I want it trimmed with violets', or pansies, or the like. Miss L was very cross and one day Jessie A was waiting for a hat to be finished and swinging back and fore on a rocking chair. A kitten got below the rocker and there was such a noise and she got such a scolding that she refused to go back.

My father and mother went most Wednesdays to the prayer meeting and we were left to our own devices. On one such occasion we started up an argument about which of us was strongest and bravest. Willie said that he could hit me so hard that I wouldn't be able to bear it and I accepted the challenge. I stood with my back to the dresser and he stood alongside. He closed his fist, drew back his arm and brought his fist full circle on to my chest. I fainted. Probably I was only stunned and breathless but the consternation was terrific. With much admired but not disinterested nobility I agreed to say nothing about it. I knew very well that I would have to bear most of the blame.

By the time I was seven or eight years old I was so convinced of my responsibility for other people's souls that I sent Alice Davidson in one day to ask her mother if she was saved. I waited at the gate for the answer. It was, 'I hope so.' One Christmas morning Alice brought out a doll her uncle had given her and displayed it proudly. I had no doll, not a grand one at any rate, but I suggested that I had better things to do than play with dolls. I recited a poem I had learnt. The first verse was:

> I little thought when last we met
> Thy sun on earth was nearly set:
> I said what I can ne'er forget,
> 'Dear boy, we'll meet again'.

Alice generously admitted my superiority, but the horrid thing about that story is that I was bitterly jealous of her for having the beautiful doll, though I would have died sooner than admit it.

As a rule, however, our intercourse was far from being on that lofty plane. We rang people's bells, invaded their gardens and were guilty of all kinds of impertinences of which our parents never dreamed. We spent one blissful afternoon investigating Wallfield House. Surrounded by a high wall and extensive grounds, it occupied the whole of that area which is now Wallfield Crescent and Wallfield Place. The occupant had died and the place was open to prospective buyers. The house was crowded with people and nobody noticed us, so we examined the place from attic to cellar; not a carpet or a piece of furniture escaped our attention.

There was a girl in Belvidere Street who for no reason at all was our enemy. When we met we made rude remarks to each other. One summer evening we saw her sitting at an upstairs window and put out our tongues at her. She immediately came after us and chased us through the Park. I made with all speed for home and arrived there breathless. My mother was alone and in genial humour and she gave me a glass of milk and a diamond-shaped sugar rice biscuit. My throat was tight and the biscuit dry with the knowledge that if my mother had known all I wouldn't have been sitting peacefully there.

Alice was bad and knew it and didn't care who else knew, but I alas hid my badness very carefully. She surprised me very much one day by saying that if she wanted her brother Arthur to play with her she said, "Go away Arthur, I don't want you' but if she didn't want him to play she pled with him and coaxed him and knew he wouldn't come. I was eminently capable of such devious practices but I wouldn't have admitted it.

We had a most memorable adventure one afternoon when Alice suggested that we should leave the Victoria Park and go to the Favourite Fieldie. It lay between Westburn Road and what is now the Sick Children's Hospital and there was a fine burn running through it. When we got there we found that we weren't alone. A boy much bigger than ourselves was there pushing himself up and down the stream on a home-made raft. He invited us to play with him and we had a wonderful time. We took off our boots and stockings – strictly forbidden. People like us didn't go about barefoot. We gathered wild flowers and played at housies and shoppies. The boy must have gone home with his raft for we waded up and down the burn. In what seemed quite a short time we remembered that we hadn't had our tea and with some difficulty forced our stockings and boots on our wet and swollen feet. By the time we set off for home it was getting surprisingly dark. Where the Westburn Park now is there was a high wall, so the road was eerie; the gate of the Victoria Park was locked and there was nothing for it but the long way round by Watson Street. We saw a man in the distance and our hearts turned over. It was Saturday night and doubtless he would be drunk but it turned out to be my father, sent out to look for us after closing the shop at 10 pm. Mr Davidson was an engineer at sea and wasn't available. We walked home soberly, one on each side of him and all he said was, 'Your mother's gey annoyed at you.' It was an understatement. Next day at Sunday School Alice boasted loudly about the thrashing she got; I don't think I was thrashed but the atmosphere would have been enough.

Sustained by Righteousness

Thrashings were unusual in our house, administered on serious occasions, but my mother was a stern disciplinarian. A back answer brought a resounding slap on the side of the head, and she had a fine repertoire of grim texts and quotations for other shortcomings. For any sign of deceitfulness there was 'Thou God seest me', a comforting text in its own setting but to us suggestive of relentless unceasing vigilance. No exaggerations or jokesome prevarications were allowed; 'A lie in fun goes to Hell in earnest,' quoted as having been said by my grandfather, saw to that.

There was constant talk of poverty but we were well dressed and sufficiently fed. If there were no extras, righteousness sustained us. There were of course no pictures – cinemas. We weren't allowed to go to concerts, or to dances or theatres, and with two exceptions we didn't go on holiday. Some of our friends got a Saturday ha'penny or penny: we didn't but a good many pennies came our way from visitors and relatives, and we weren't too conscientious about putting them in our Savings Banks. Ice cream was not common as it is now. It was forbidden; being made by Italians it was probably dirty, and their shops were known to be dens of iniquity. Only at the Sunday School picnic did we spend our few pennies on 'sliders'.

A woman, Sowens Jean, with two pails of sowens, used to come down the street occasionally, and people went out with jugs to buy some but we never did – again it might be dirty. Neither did we buy buckies. That didn't worry us, the sight of them being picked out with a pin and eaten was enough. And there was dulse, too, but our squeamish tastes revolted at it. German bands, barrel organs with monkeys, and dancing bears provided street entertainment. We followed them from street to street in spite of being told that dreadful cruelties were inflicted on the bears to make them dance.

We didn't have parties in our house, but Mr and Mrs Cable always gave one at Christmas and so did Auntie Jeannie, and sometimes Auntie Agnes. The Cables had no family but a great many children gathered about them and they gave lavish parties. We were encouraged to eat and drink and boast how many iced cakes we had had. Arthur Bruce held the record when he ate thirteen. When we were asked to sing, Jessie A and I gave our rendering of my mother's favourite hymn:

Your Father and I

I hear the words of love
I gaze upon the blood
I see the mighty sacrifice
And I have peace with God.

We thought we were singing a duet. Actually we both sang the air. She was the better singer, and I supplied the aplomb.

Lemonade and ginger beer were unusual luxuries, but we drank liquorice-water of our own manufacture. We bought a stick of liquorice from the chemist, cut it into small pieces and shook it up in a bottle of water. This dreadful brew then became public property. We were constantly warned by mother never to drink liquorice water out of Janetie Morton's bottle; Janetie was a poor little thing, she said, and it would be very mean to take anything away from her. The Mortons left Thomson Street and went to stay at the top house of Cairnfield Place. I went frequently to play with Janetie. She was big-eyed, pale and emaciated and sat in an armchair wrapped in shawls and blankets. I sat close beside her and we played at Ludo and made pictures with blocks. She died of consumption before she was ten.

There were two families of Morgans on our street – not related to each other. The James Morgan family was on terms of intimacy with some of our relations, they were Baptists. The oldest son was studying for the Baptist ministry. He had some kind of growth cut off his head, it stood in a tumbler on the kitchen mantelpiece for several days and was displayed to visitors. Polly was my contemporary. She had St Vitus Dance and if she was contradicted she flew into a frenzy of rage and went around the room kicking everything she could reach. She was nevertheless a pious child, and we were conducting a service together one day when Jessie A came in and announced that Auntie Maggie in Edinburgh, Charlie's wife, had got a baby girl. Jack, their son, was four years old by this time.

Babies were no novelty to us. All our neighbours had them and we had steadily arriving cousins and second cousins. When Jessie A and I had whooping-cough my father made leather purses for us and put some coppers in them. I thought that on the same principle if mothers were ill the doctor gave them a baby as a present, and the more ill they were the more likely the doctor was to reward them. Going alone with my father to church on a Sunday morning I said, 'Neddie Pollock's mother has a new baby and she had only a sore throat. That wasn't very much, was it?' 'No,' he said, 'it wasn't very much' and something in his tone and look told me that I had made a silly remark.

Then there was my visit to Mrs Reid. We went frequently to see her. She had been housekeeper to Uncle John at Tullynessle when he was a widower, and my mother had kept up the friendship though Jessie A and I did most of the visiting. It was like going to see another grandmother. Mrs Reid's husband was a policeman, a queer taciturn man, and there was a clever, almost grown-up family. On this particular day while friends and families were being discussed she said to me, 'Does your mother think Mrs Boddie is wearing the long cloak?' The expression meant nothing to me and indeed I have never heard it since but I passed it on when I went home. That evening Aunts Lizzie and Jessie were in and I overheard my mother telling them in whispers about it. They seemed amused and she said, 'I never heard anything so ridiculous, Mrs Reid must have taken leave of her senses.' I set the two incidents together in my mind for future consideration.

The other Morgan family were interesting but different. The mother was Highland, soft-spoken and pleasant and a byword for dirt and general incompetence. There was a story that one Sunday she burnt the broth; nobody would eat it and nobody would clean the burnt pot. So it stood in the middle of the kitchen floor for a week. At the side of the kitchen fireplace there was a heap of clothes waiting to be mended. It reached to the mantelpiece. I suggested to Tilda – we must have been alone in the house – that we would tidy it up but she laughed and said, 'That's Mother's corner, it is never tidied up.' Mrs Morgan, however, was a kind and generous soul. Once every summer she gathered the children on the street and took us for a picnic to Barclay's Wood. It was a belt of trees on the edge of Raeden. There were very few houses beyond the Victoria Park and it was an excursion into the country, and we spent a long afternoon at it. Mr Morgan, who was our landlord and owned a good many of the houses on the street, was a stranger to his family. They said he never spoke to them and they never dreamt of accosting him. They weren't afraid of him, just indifferent.

That was incomprehensible to us. When our father turned into the street we tore up to meet him, told him everything we had been doing and knew that he would never give us away. On summer Sunday afternoons when there was no Sunday School he took us for walks and taught us to distinguish one tree from another and to recognise the various crops in the fields. On Trades Holidays we went further afield and I remember going to Dunnottar Castle and being shown the conglomerate rocks. My mother didn't come with us. Possibly Charlie was too young, but it wasn't the kind of thing she bothered about.

I have no recollection of learning to read – probably I did so along with Jessie A who was a year ahead of me. Neither do I remember being read to, though my mother was almost certain to have read to us. One thing I do remember – if Jessie A or I got new books we couldn't wait a minute to read them separately. We read each book together – she would read so many pages, and then I read an equal number so that neither had any advantage over the other. This plan eventually fell to pieces because we were both so vain and deceitful. Each of us would rather have read the whole book than yield to the other so we marked a place for stopping. When Jessie A read XYZ I knew my turn had come. But Satan stepped in – XYZ was omitted from the reading and Jessie A or myself sailed on. The end was inevitable.

We never seemed to be ill-off for something to read. My father had a fairish collection of heavily bound books – Scott, Dickens, church history, bound volumes of *Good Words, The Quiver* and the *Sunday at Home* – all grist to the mill. There was also a steadily increasing number of biographies – Samuel Rutherford, Murray McCheyne – and missionary books. The showpiece of our library, however, was a large fully illustrated *Pilgrim's Progress*. My father had bought it in instalments and got it bound. There was also in the kitchen a big framed picture of a man asleep on a couch, and underneath in ornamental letters 'As I Slept I Dreamed'. Every Sunday the *Pilgrim's Progress* was on display and we knew all the pictures by heart. We got the *Christian Herald* every week and read it from cover to cover. There was always a good serial story, a sermon by CH Spurgeon or Dr Talmage. Believe it or not, I read them and still remember bits of them, paragraphs setting forth strange incidents with a text, not always appropriate, at the end. But the most thrilling of all, *Baxter's Prophecies*. Baxter, whoever he was, prophesied frequently that the end of the world was at hand, and very often a definite date was mentioned.

One day at the dinner hour I went down George Street to a shop where we could buy locust beans. I believe they were meant for horses but they were cheap and sweet and eatable. When I came out of the shop there was a strange darkness. It was happening! Baxter was right and this was the end of the world, but it was only an eclipse of the sun.

School seems to have little place in my recollections. We went first to Rosemount School, but when fees were stopped and children from Short Loanings and Leadside Road came to it our parents thought it would be too rough for us and we were sent to the C of S Normal School where Auntie Jessie was a pupil-teacher. Jessie A abhorred Rosemount School and had a teacher who terrified her, but I remember nothing about it except that I wore a print dress, blue and white striped, on my first day. I have no unhappy thoughts about school. Lessons gave me no trouble, I didn't dislike my teachers and such things as I remember have little connection with either. My Aunt Mary died in Edinburgh when I was in the First Standard, now Primary 3. We, the children, knew her very little; the memorable thing is that we were dressed in mourning – black serge dresses trimmed with black velvet and with huge puffs in the sleeves. It was the custom so we weren't odd – envied rather.

The road to school was long but direct, straight down Rosemount Place and Maberly Street. In the morning Maberly Street was crowded with mill-girls coming from Broadford. They started work at 5 or 6 am. They all wore shawls over their heads and shoulders, and there was a prevailing dusty but pleasant smell of hemp. At the top of Skene Square there was a shop where we bought pomegranates at a halfpenny each. I doubt whether I have ever tasted one since. One winter we passed Skene Square School with fear and trembling. Rumour had it that Jack the Ripper had been seen in the playground lavatories.

Home was more interesting than school. We had lots of visitors and they all had their own fascination. After Uncle James Stewart's death Auntie of Montgarrie came to town

37

occasionally and stayed with my grandmother but made a kind of royal progress round all the other households. Her advent was regarded with awed excitement; everybody was prepared to hear home truths, pleasant and otherwise, but nobody would have dared to object; Auntie was Auntie and that was enough. She was a quaint figure in bonnet, dolman and voluminous skirts. She carried a large carpet bag with odds and ends but her garments were all on her person; they said she even wore her nightgown under her dress, only for the journey of course, to save packing and to provide warmth in the train. To the great indignation of Lizzie and Jessie she sat in my grandmother's chair, got first read of the newspaper and commanded the whole situation.

My mother and she greeted each other with great affection, spoke endlessly about Midward, and wept a good deal. When she finally left for home the parting scene afforded us great pleasure. As the final moment drew near they got more and more tearful and at last in floods of tears said farewell. As long as she was in sight Auntie turned and turned again waving her hand and saying 'God be with you till we meet again'.

We were still in Rosemount Place when my grandmother and the aunts gave a party for all the grandchildren. For the guests it was a supremely happy occasion; not so for the hostesses. It so happened that Auntie of Montgarrie was there on one of her visits and she was at her most Auntie-ish. She didn't mingle with the revellers but sat in the kitchen the picture of woe. Tears ran down her face whilst she shook her head from side to side saying, 'What would my dear Charlie have said to a scene like this?' Assurances that the party was completely innocent and a family affair only brought psalms and hymns and poems, the most impressive beginning 'If now the Judge were at the door, whom all mankind must stand before', and ending 'Shall we with fiends or angels dwell?' It was generally felt that really Auntie had gone too far.

Perhaps our favourite visitor was Uncle Tom, the only one of my father's brothers we really knew. Uncle George had been an invalid for some time before he died and had never meant much to us. Uncles Alex and David were both in Canada, and James had died young. Uncle Tom had a merchant's shop in Culter and used to bring apples which he cut for us in a fancy pattern, and at

Christmas he sent us all kinds of Christmas fare. When he came in he always said, 'How many pandies did you get today?' 'None', we would say. 'Nine', he held up his hands in horror, 'Not any' with great emphasis. 'Not many? I would call nine a good lot.' He was the only person who called me Tubbie.

James Morrice, a cousin of my grandfather, came once a year and stayed for a night. He was a tall old man, quite bald and clean-shaven except for white whiskers from ear to ear under his chin. He was supposed to be very deaf but had a disconcerting habit of replying if somebody spoke in a whisper. We had great difficulty in averting our eyes from him at dinner time because when he ate his ears went round and round in circles. Jessie A and I once spent a weekend at his farm at Arnage. His daughter kept house for him, her husband worked the farm and they had children of our age. There was no church near them and James took us on Sunday afternoon to a hall where a minister of the Episcopal Church was preaching. He explained to his stolid Presbyterian audience the significance of all his vestments. On the way home James made only one remark: 'That man said the white thing was the robe of righteousness, but when he turned roon I noticed there was a big hole in't'.

Willie Smith, son of Uncle John of the shop, with his two children always spent New Year's Day with us. His wife had died when Jimmie was a baby. They came in time for dinner and stayed till after tea. My father and he were kindred spirits; they both had a keen sense of the ridiculous and entertained each other immensely. My mother and he were the best of friends but he was *non persona grata* with the other members of the Smith family. For one thing he had when he was a very young man been depressed – 'melancholy' was the word then used – and had been for a short time in the Asylum. For another, his wife had not been socially acceptable: she had relations who worked in the mills. And worst of all, he had been known to make slighting remarks about the Gordon Mission. He was well educated and clever, and had written a history of the Vale of Alford, and a history of the Clan Forbes. Both of them were highly thought of, and he also contributed poems to several periodicals.

Another person who was unacceptable to the relations was Mrs Law, Maggie Smith of Auchmar. The slight simplicity that marked the rest of the Auchmar family reached its peak in her, she really was simple, though she was an excellent housekeeper and brought up an intelligent and well-doing family. She had disgraced the whole family connection by having an illegitimate son. Our branch of the Smith family couldn't forget it and extended their coolness to the Laws, but my mother who deplored sinfulness in all its manifestations couldn't manage to be unkind to the sinners. She liked people of all kinds, except my father's relations.

Maggie Smith had been on the point of marrying the father of her child. Her parents were driving with her to Aberdeen to buy the wedding garments when a young woman ran out of a cottage at the roadside and told them that she had an equal right to be the bride. Uncle William turned the horse's head and made for home and there was no wedding. He and Aunt Betsy adopted the baby and brought him up as their own and Maggie consoled herself in no time at all by marrying George Law. She was noted for making fatuous remarks like 'Eh Jessie, you're awful like your mother, or is't your father you're like?' and 'Eh, Helen, we're aa sinners but there's nane o us sinners like Jock Robertson' – presumably he was one of her boy-friends. Her sister Mary Ann was very different. She was brisk and managing, and could shake hands so as to leave a penny in one's palm. It was a knack we admired and vainly tried to acquire.

In 1897 we left Thomson Street and went to Rosemount Place. My father had taken a shop in a new building at the top of Argyll Place and we occupied a flat above it. It is easy to fix the date because we settled in just before Queen Victoria's Diamond Jubilee. Like every other town in the country Aberdeen went all gay and there was a tremendous procession. We were very important. Being on the route of the procession we could invite all our friends to come and look.

Benches were arranged in the shop window like a grandstand and employees and acquaintances were accommodated there. The elite, meaning the relations, viewed from the windows of the house and were regaled with tea and cakes. The celebrations were on a scale hitherto unknown, but the only thing I remember is that Mary Queen of Scots was represented by Miss Stephen, one of our teachers at the Normal School. She was handsome and accomplished and later on a new headmaster was said to be in love with her. His name was Duncan Mackenzie and one day when he went into her classroom she was beginning a singing lesson and started up 'Duncan Gray cam here to woo. Ha! Ha! the wooin o't!' It was said that he was done with women for ever after.

Life had a different pattern for us after we left Thomson Street. Jessie A and I continued our friendships with the chums there, some of them till long after we were grown up but we never had friends in Rosemount Place. Perhaps our playing days were over. There were a lot of boys around who made playmates for Willie and Charlie. They would have been nine and six respectively when the Boer War began. The war didn't seem to matter much to us; we had no soldiers amongst us, and except that we recited rhymes about Kruger and added words like Kopye and bomb and khaki to our vocabulary it left us untouched.

Willie and Charlie, but especially Charlie, lived in the war. From morning till night battles raged, and bruises and cuts were the order of the day. If Charlie was asked to account for torn clothes he said they had been destroyed by the Boers at Spion Kop or in the siege of Ladysmith. My mother, I think, showed too little patience with him. His imaginations were apt to be called lies, and his casualties wanton destruction.

Then Queen Victoria died and the world seemed to have fallen to pieces. Everyone went into mourning; even children like us got black hats. The pulpit in church was draped in black and for a long time a congregation looked like a sea of black, not a colour to be seen anywhere. I can't speak for the country in general but amongst our kind of people there was no enthusiasm for Edward as a King. All his amorous adventures, appearances in divorce courts and so on were freely discussed. We got Coronation mugs and medals at school but I remember nothing about the event, only that it was postponed because Edward had appendicitis. Nobody had heard the word before but they supposed it was what had been known as 'inflammation of the bowels'.

We didn't stay very long in Rosemount Place. The house was too small and the street too noisy so we went to Richmond Terrace. Before that, however, Jessie A had been taken away from school, at the age of 12. In retrospect this seems a foolish move, and at the time the relations weren't pleased, but there were circumstances that explained it. First of all, Uncle Tom had died. The day of his funeral my father had a severe haemorrhage and my mother was quite certain that this was the first of a succession of shocks – three was supposed to be the number – that would finish him. Jessie A must therefore be put into the shop so that 'somebody of his own' would be near him. Incidentally Uncle Tom had left half his not very large estate to be divided amongst his surviving brothers. In view of what later happened amongst the Smiths it is of interest that the brothers voluntarily divided the money with Uncle George's girls.

The other deciding factor was that Jessie A was very unhappy at school. She wasn't stupid and in fact kept at the top of her class – nobody in our house, except Charlie, would have dared to do anything else – but she was afraid of teachers and couldn't get on with other girls. Though younger, I was frequently told to ask so-and-so why she had ill-used Jessie A. My mother was desperate and thought there was nothing for it but to let her stay at home. The experiment wasn't a success. How could it have been? She was in the shop when she was wanted in the house and in the house when she was wanted in the shop. She escaped when possible in the afternoon to meet me at the school gate and accompany me and my friends home. After a year or so she was sent to classes and then to work in an office.

Our cousin Margaret Morrice came over from Canada about this time. She was a delegate to a Sunday School Convention in London and came to Aberdeen to make the acquaintance of the relatives. Uncle Alex and Uncle David were both dead. David had never married. Alex was my father's oldest brother and had married young so his family belonged to an older generation than ours. We were interested to have first-hand news about our cousins and their families. One of them, William, was at that time Chief Constable of Rochester NY and he had two sons, one a university lecturer and the other in the Admiralty offices in Washington. Margaret was a nurse and wore a Red Cross badge. She was the same age as my mother and a woman after her own heart. The Morrice stock rose considerably. During the 1914–18 war a sister, Jessie, came over with the Canadians. She spent her leaves in Aberdeen and once with us in Cromarty and was as satisfactory as Margaret.

Sustained by Righteousness

There was a time when moral disaster stared our family in the face. The fear of having sons given over to crime haunted my mother. Willie and Charlie and two of their friends began to play football. They hadn't a ball and couldn't get any of the parents to provide one, so they headed a sheet of paper 'Argyll Football Club' and went down Argyll Place collecting for a football. They got 2s 9d, not enough, so they spent it on sweeties. In those days 2s 9d bought a lot of sweeties, so discovery was speedy and retribution speedier. Even my father was called in to administer chastisement. It must have been Willie's only experience of punishment. He was very docile and good but if he did need correction my mother found that she couldn't lay a hand on him, because he roared so horribly. He sounded like a dumb animal, she said, and she was reminded of the years when she was afraid he would never speak. I mentioned this to Willie lately and he said he didn't remember it but had no doubt it was a well-calculated effort on his part.

Charlie, on the other hand, took punishment as his daily bread; he was never out of trouble. In his imagination at any rate he waged a constant war with the two policemen on the beat; neither of them ever caught up with him. When he saw one of them in the distance he made for home, being sure that retribution for ringing bells or hanging on the back of tramcars was going to overtake him. When he arrived breathless, my mother would order him to sit there for an hour and maybe he would learn to behave himself. In ten minutes he would plead 'Thrash me, and let me get out'. No consideration of irreverence would keep him from referring to the two policemen as Bible Feet and Testament Toes respectively. My father thought him infinitely amusing and witty.

By the time we were living in Richmond Terrace we were leaving childhood behind. I went to the Central School and then at 14 to be a pupil-teacher. Willie and Charlie in their turn left school and went into offices. Willie wanted desperately to stay on at school, but as his speech was still difficult my mother thought the ministry unsuitable and that was the only profession she was interested in.

4

SURROUNDED

We were now closely surrounded by our relations. Uncle Charlie had left Edinburgh and was with his family in Whitehall Place. Grandma and the aunts were in Mid Stocket Road, Uncle Willie in Westburn Road, and Uncle James further down the same road, At close quarters they were oppressive.

Uncle Charlie didn't stay long in Aberdeen but went to S Africa leaving Auntie Maggie and the children in Whitehall Place. He was dour and queer but his least admiring friends never accused him of being quarrelsome. He simply withdrew into grim silence. It would have been difficult to quarrel with Auntie Maggie. She found people an amusing study and wouldn't have bothered to quarrel with anybody. Nevertheless Uncle Charlie's absence was something of a relief all round. My grandmother unfortunately had started them off on the wrong foot when they came to Aberdeen by saying to Auntie Maggie that she hoped Charlie would dress well for the sake of his brothers. This was not only tactless but quite unnecessary since he was the best-looking and best-dressed of all her sons.

Charlie's son, Jack, was showing signs of being as peculiar as his father but in the opposite direction. He never stopped speaking, had no reticences and couldn't be snubbed. At his approach people ran to lock their parlour doors to keep him from playing their organs and pianos – mostly organs because they were more suitable for hymns – and he had even been known to mount a lorry on the street at a flitting and give musical selections from the organ on it.

Charlie Smith, son of Uncle Willie and Auntie Jeannie, started his apprenticeship as an engineer and spent every Sunday afternoon and evening with us, went to church with us and joined Rutherford Church. We were always on the best of terms with Uncle Willie's family but they had arrived at seven-yearly intervals, so Charlie was the only one old enough to find us

44

companionable. He had been brought up to go to the Gordon Mission and his going to church with us was looked upon with disfavour by Uncle James and his satellites. Charlie's parents wouldn't have minded but Uncle James had to be placated.

Every Thursday when Auntie Maggie posted her letter to Uncle Charlie she spent the afternoon with my mother. Jack and Ella called in for her on their way home from school. They were kindred spirits and had a wonderful time discussing the relations, Auntie Maggie with humour, and my mother with more indignation than amusement. Of the five households, we two went to church, the other three went to the Gordon Mission. We went under compulsion to special meetings at the Mission. Uncle James was liable to call in and remark that he hadn't seen any of us if we didn't.

Altogether there were plenty of topics for Thursday afternoons. Auntie Jeannie was natural and honest to the point of vulgarity and impertinence. Sometimes she was so popular with the aunts that they had no time for anybody else. Uncle Willie and she were generous and hospitable, addicted to grand parties and expensive holidays, and at these times they were useful friends. Auntie Jeannie was tactless, however, and made remarks like 'You should see what a cheap ugly carpet so and so has, just like that one you have in your sitting room'. Then there would be a spell of coldness between the aunts and Jeannie, and we would have a temporary popularity with Jeannie and Willie. At these times their generosity became extravagance, inexcusable in view of the past – meaning Auntie of Montgarrie's £70. Jeannie neglected her family, the aunts would say, and did nothing but gallivant and enjoy herself. Uncle Willie and Auntie Jeannie certainly enjoyed themselves and weren't too enslaved to their family. If Uncle Willie went on a long trip, to Wick or the Orkneys, Auntie Jeannie thought nothing of shutting up the house, sending the family to Alford to stay with her mother, and being away for a month or more. School was of no account at all. She dressed in the extreme of fashion and spoke of her Paris Models. When bicycles became fashionable she was amongst the first to ride one and to wear divided skirts. At a time when ladies of fashion limped because Queen Alexandra had had an illness that left her lame, Auntie Jeannie went about with a shepherd's crook. 'Preserve me Jeannie,' said my grandmother, 'have you hurt your leg?'

Uncle Charlie came home from S Africa after a few years, stayed for a year and then went to California. He was no more cheerful than before but inclined to be superior, having seen more of the world than his relations. He came a good deal to our house, the only place where he got sympathy, but I can't remember that he ever spoke to anybody but my mother. Again his departure was unregretted.

The aunts at Mid Stocket were getting uppish and dressy and resented having nieces who weren't so very much younger than themselves. We were useful to them for doing messages but were apt to be left on the doorstep when they had grander company within. Friends who frequented our house automatically got a cold reception in theirs. When the Laws came one by one to the town to jobs or to college, they spent all their spare time with us. Gordon came straight to the Free Press office when he finished at Fordyce Academy. Having paid a duty call at Mid Stocket, been asked what pay he was getting –it was 14s weekly –and told that he could be saving some of it, he regarded them with loathing.

Fortunately there was only one point at which their lives touched ours but it was a vulnerable one. When they were pleased to be gracious my mother was pathetically happy; if they withdrew their favour she searched her heart and household for reasons. She never could be indifferent. They would have hated to know that all their reactions to their many relations were known to us because my grandmother told me all on my Saturday morning visits.

They may have been annoying but were never really diverting. Their sisters-in-law were. James' wife, Auntie Agnes, was never a favourite but because of Uncle James she had to be tholed and even pandered to. In their early days when he was still an itinerant evangelist and went away for two or three weeks at a time she expected one of the aunts to go down and stay with her overnight. This became an intolerable nuisance but when Uncle James took to hinting to my grandmother that his sisters might be more attentive to Agnes in his absence, they realised that she had pretended she was alone. They didn't dare to disillusion him but when Isa came home on holiday she undertook the job. She went down every night for a week, then bided her time till she knew Uncle James was at home and paid them a visit. 'Oh Agnes,' she said as she rose to go, 'I left my bedroom slippers when I was down sleeping here last week', and seeing the looks that passed was satisfied that she left trouble behind her.

Uncle James' full name was James Alexander and for some reason connected with his wife's delusions of grandeur he was henceforth known to all his connections as JA. She seemed to be incapable of straightforward behaviour. She would call on my mother or Auntie Maggie, work the conversation round to some topic of family interest and question them closely about it. Then they would be furious to discover that she knew more about it than they did and was simply checking up. But she didn't carry tales. There was no frankness in her anywhere. She was also incredibly mean. She gave presents that were exhibited and laughed over endlessly. Once she gave my grandmother as a Christmas gift a kettle-holder she had got in a penny dip at a bazaar, and one of the aunts found her shamelessly tying up cheap chocolates in the wrappings and box she had carefully preserved when someone gave her an expensive gift. This, she explained, was for one of her nieces.

But her chief characteristic was grandeur. She knew only the best people. There was the circle of county people and well-to-do townspeople who had started the Gordon Mission at a time when there was a lack of gospel-preaching in remote country districts and in the town slums. Her English accent and ladylike appearance evidently made her acceptable to these people and she cultivated their acquaintance assiduously. This commended her to the aunts but they weren't so sure about another manifestation of her seclusiveness. Agnes' daughter Guin, till she was old enough to go to school, was dressed in Kate Greenaway fashion. I remember her with a red velvet smocked dress reaching to her heels and a poke bonnet to match. The aunts could stand a lot of grandeur but that was going too far.

Auntie Agnes was Episcopalian. It was whispered among the relatives that her daughter Guin as a young girl was confirmed in the C of E when she was staying with her grandparents. She certainly is C of E now (1961) and much involved with organisations in her local church. She has no love that I know of for the Gordon Mission. After her mother left Aberdeen and she, Guin, spent an occasional weekend at 178 she went always, accompanied by Isa, to St Ninian's or Beechgrove (C of S churches). I

47

always suspected that Isa was glad of the chance. (Guin, baptised Ethel Violet Guinevere Smith, became a doctor – Aberdeen University 1921 – and was for many years a medical officer with Barnardo Homes).

My brother Charlie refused to go to the Gordon Mission. He made no objection to church-going and went with his chums to Sunday School and Bible Class but he made no secret of his dislike for Uncle James and all that he stood for. There were constant hints from the relations that Charlie wasn't all that he might be, and my mother admitted to them that she found him difficult.

Willie had never given up his intention of going to the University and spent all his spare time studying for Prelims, so Charlie and he didn't go about together or have the same friends, but they were always on the best of terms. Charlie kept an eye on Willie's appearance and was particular about his own. He insisted that they both got bowler hats which they wore on Sundays, and Charlie occasionally donned one when he went out of an evening. In course of time Willie remarked that it was very odd that his hat looked shabby whereas Charlie's, which was worn often, looked quite fresh. The explanation was simple. Charlie wore his own hat on Sundays but Willie's on weekdays. It was typical of his sense of humour and everybody was amused except my mother. Poor Charlie, he was so gay and so handsome and popular but he wasn't like the Smiths. He played well by ear but was never trained, he was a lovely singer but wasn't allowed to sing songs in the house. If he brought in his friends they played card games so they were forbidden the house. There was no question at all of gambling – cards were 'the Devil's playthings' and a live tiger would have been as welcome as a pack of cards.

My engagement to your father did nothing to improve the increasingly strained relations with the Mid Stocket aunts. Since I was only 17 that was perhaps not surprising, but for once my mother stood no nonsense from her sisters. Uncle Willie and Auntie Jeannie and Auntie Maggie were as usual all kindness and hospitality, but it was a long time before your father and I were invited to make an evening call at Mid Stocket. Auntie of Montgarrie was there on one of her visits; she was on her best behaviour and your father and she took an immediate fancy to each other. We were never at any time invited to Uncle James' house; the fact that your father was studying for the ministry did not commend him there, but I had great difficulty in convincing him of that.

Soon after this Auntie Annie came home. The lady to whom she had been lady's maid and companion for twenty years had died and left her some money. My grandmother was getting old and the idea seemed to be that Annie would stay at Mid Stocket and help with the housekeeping. She made dresses inexpertly and expensively for her relations and kept herself occupied, but she wasn't happy and neither was Grandma. Lizzie and Jessie, never noted for tact, praised everything she did as if nothing had ever been properly done before. Auntie Annie was kind and gentle and wouldn't have harmed a fly. She found the whole situation intolerable. It wasn't long before she made her escape.

Her engagement to James Cameron, a newly-made widower with six of a family, was hailed with all the enthusiasm which had been lacking from mine – except from my grandmother, who never reconciled herself to Annie's marriage. Mr Cameron was a Plymouth Brother and had plenty of money. Lizzie and Jessie were annoyed at my grandmother's lack of enthusiasm and said to her, 'You're ready enough to tease Bella Morrice' – she didn't –'but you never say anything nice to Annie'. 'Oh,' she said meekly, 'I didn't understand that I was expected to make fun with Annie about Cameron. I'll wait till his wife is cold in her grave.' When he had been a widower for a year the marriage took place in Edinburgh by special licence. Thereafter the Cameron family took first place with the aunts, and all the aunts' nieces and nephews were expected to fall in behind them.

General Black (son of a cousin of Charles Smith, of Midward: see p6) died and left some money amongst the Smiths, £100 to each widow – Charles, John and William were all dead – and to Auntie of Montgarrie, and £100 to the eldest son in each family. The money wasn't to be paid over till his sister died and then there would be a further £100 to each of them from her estate. This didn't make much stir in the family till Auntie of Montgarrie died and then it became known that Uncle James had drawn up a will for her by which he was the chief legatee. Trifling sums were left to Auntie Annie, as her namesake, and to John Smith of Auchmar. Cousin Willie Smith, whom she had brought up, wasn't mentioned at all in the will. I don't know what money she left, probably only the General's £100. There was a good deal of murmuring amongst some members of the family. Willie Smith was bitterly hurt that Auntie had passed him by, especially as he was already showing signs of a recurrence of melancholia. The Auchmar family, John Smith's, preserved a discreet silence, but when John Smith eventually got his cheque, which wasn't till after Miss Black died, he signed it and posted it at once to the Gordon Mission.

My mother was staggered, not because she didn't get money. She complained about poverty but wouldn't have put 'her heel for her toe', to use a saying of my grandmother's, to get a penny that didn't come to her naturally. But that JA the paragon, should have so demeaned himself! She tried to suggest to herself that perhaps he felt the money was due to him because of his having paid the £70 debt of long ago to Auntie, but her idol was beginning to show signs of having feet of clay. She was increasingly aware that he was not all that she had imagined him to be. I have no doubt at all that he had been quite a nice youth and had deteriorated. Then, to find that, far from her meaning a lot to JA, he was so indifferent to her that he could cheat her out of her mother's money nearly killed her.

I went to Rothiemay in 1908, taught there for a year and a half, and was married and went to Nethybridge in 1910. From that time I didn't stay at home except for holidays and my news of it is apt to be secondhand. Whilst I was finding new interests in Nethybridge and then in Contin and Cromarty, life wasn't too prosperous for the family in Aberdeen. My father had a very severe heart attack just before I was married. He gave up the business and for the remaining two years of his life was more or less invalided. He had frequent and distressing heart attacks, but never failed in patience and good humour. When he died in July 1912 aged 75 the doctor said to my mother, 'That was the sweetest old man I ever met'.

With his quietening influence gone the situation worsened. The words 'neurosis' and 'adolescence' were not in common use then but Jessie A suffered from the one and my brother Charlie from the other. My mother was really to be pitied. Jessie A got up at an unearthly hour in the morning and tore about cleaning. At dinner time she ate ravenously and then was sick. When she came home at night she burst into tears as soon as she entered the house and would then spend the evening in a round of visits, at the choir practice or the Guild. And worst of all, every now and again she retired to bed for a fortnight. The doctor, when appealed to, just said, 'She's a poor nervous thing,' and left it at that.

In February of 1913 my grandmother died. I was by then in Cromarty. My mother and Willie went to the funeral. Willie went out to Tullynessle with the uncles and mother waited at Mid Stocket till they came back. Then after tea Uncle James read the will. He had done for my grandmother what he did for Auntie of Montgarrie, drawn up a will and made himself the chief beneficiary. At this distance of time I don't remember the exact figures but he came first, then John, then Lizzie and Jessie equal; to Annie, Charlie, Isa and my mother the princely sum of £3 each; to Willie nothing because he had a legacy of his own, being the eldest son. In fact Uncle James had the effrontery to say that if he had been in Willie's place he would have divided the legacy with the rest of the family. Miss Black was still alive, but he had provisionally divided her money too, £30 each to John and himself, and £20 each to Jessie and Lizzie.

All this was bad enough but what my mother could never forgive was that before the will was read Uncle James prayed that the memory of their sainted father would prevent them from bickering and ill-feeling. When the reading was finished she stood up and said to my brother Willie, 'We'll go home now,' and left the company without another word. Nor did she ever mention the will to any member of the family.

Miss Black died very shortly afterwards but her lawyers refused to divide the second £100 according to the will. Since grandmother predeceased Miss Black it wasn't hers to divide, so it was divided equally amongst them.

There is an interesting sequel to that story. JA, John, Lizzie and Jessie put their money into a building society of which a certain Baillie Kemp, known to them, was treasurer. He absconded shortly after, taking all the Society's money with him and they lost every penny. Uncle Willie and Auntie Jeannie had a wonderful splash with their £200. Amongst other things, everybody in the household got a brand new bicycle.

This development didn't help to reconcile Charlie to his relations or to the state of things in general, and there was worse to follow. Uncle James met him along with some of his friends in Mid Stocket one day and stopped to ask him if it wasn't time he was saved. Neither Charlie nor any of his relations ever told us what his reply was, but there was open warfare between them from that day. The aunts openly referred to him as 'that scamp', and Charlie refused to enter a room if one of them was in it. If they came in he rose and left the house. When Charlie stayed with us, as he often did after I was married, he was delightful company. At home he was intransigent to a degree. He wouldn't come in at what was considered a decent hour at night – 50 years ago any time after 10.00pm, elders' hours, was frowned upon. He refused to have his friends chosen for him or to give them up when the relations snooped around and reported that they were unsatisfactory. There were constant rows which distressed Willie, and increased Jessie A's nervousness, and then my mother issued an ultimatum – either he would conform to the rules she laid down or he must leave the house. He left it.

Willie and Jessie A were no parties to this. They thought my mother went too far, and to this day they can hardly bear to remember Charlie. On the other hand they couldn't understand why he wouldn't yield a little for the sake of peace. If he felt any bitterness he didn't show it; he frequented the house, but lived in lodgings. I don't know how long this lasted, perhaps only a few months. The war came and Charlie enlisted. He got a commission in the 1/5th Seaforths, and he liked the army – so much that he decided to make it his career. He studied for and got a commission in the Regular Army, in the Royal Engineers. He had been working for some time organising water supplies for the camps behind the lines, when at Hill 60 most of the Seaforth officers were killed. He was lent to his old battalion and was three days in the front line when along with six others he was killed by a bursting shell. Letters from his Commanding Officer and fellow subalterns spoke of him as having outstanding gifts as leader and organiser, and all of them mentioned his charming personality and popularity.

He was the only one of the family who didn't return from the war except Cousin Willie Smith's boy Jimmie who was missing and was never heard of. Charlie Smith was in the Navy, and Jack Smith came over with the Canadians; so did our cousin Jessie

Morrice. Towards the end of the war Uncle James went to France to work in a canteen run by some missionary society. He came home complaining of severe chill, got gradually worse and was a complete invalid for nearly ten years. Latterly he was so helpless that the only thing he could do to get in touch with other people was to try and make words by shuffling letters together with a little stick.

Willie Smith, who was already depressed, was quite broken down after Jimmie was reported missing believed killed. Bella was still very young and there was nobody to look after him, so he was put into Kingseat. He wasn't there very long when he took pneumonia and died. But before his death a letter came to Uncle John from, as I remember it, someone working on *The Times* asking if he could give him any information about a William Smith belonging to Alford who had written two books dealing with the history of the Alford district. He was anxious, he said, to get copies of the books because he wanted information for a book he intended to write. Uncle John replied that he understood the William Smith he mentioned was now in a mental hospital and unable to transact business and that he knew nothing about his books. When my mother heard of this she refused to believe that John was wicked enough to have done such a thing unless he was egged on by his sisters. She was chiefly concerned about Bella who was now living with her mother's people who took her away from school at the earliest possible date and sent her to work in the Grandholm Mills. She thought that if Uncle John had behaved with any decency it would have been possible to do something about getting the books and that Bella might have profited thereby. Before Willie died his £200 from the Black estate had been paid over. The Board of Managers at Kingseat, who might well have claimed the money, handed over £100 of it to Bella in token of their sympathy for her in the loss of her father and brother. My mother knew that she would have liked to go in for nursing, but hadn't enough education, and as a millworker had little prospect of being accepted by a matron. Now that she had enough money to buy the necessary outfit, they called Nurse Grant in for advice and she spoke to the Matron of Morningfield who gave her some kind of job in the hospital. It wasn't a training school, but she did so well there that the Matron could recommend her to the Matron of Woodend.

Bella Smith recently told me a story, new to me, which brought tears of shame to my eyes. For no apparent reason she said, 'When I started nursing, your mother saw to everything for me, application and uniform and so on. The first time I had an examination I got a letter from her by the morning post saying that she was remembering what an important day this was for me, and that she wouldn't forget me all day. After that I never had an exam of any importance that I hadn't a letter from her in the morning.'

By the time the war was over, my brother Willie was at the University. He graduated in Arts and then in Divinity and was licensed in 1921. He spent a year as an assistant in Dundee, and when he was called to Leitholm he took my mother and Jessie A with him to keep house. This he did to some extent unwillingly, but they were very unhappy in Aberdeen and glad to have a chance of removing themselves from so many uncongenial relations. Jessie A had, I think, the only happy years of her life in Leitholm. My mother, in spite of everything that had happened, pined for her own folk and had them all down to visit her – not Uncle James, he was quite incapacitated by that time. She died in 1926 and Willie married the following year.

After Mother and Uncle James were both dead Uncle Charlie came home on holiday. He had retired and gone to Victoria to live with his family. For some reason or other he worked in Los Angeles though it was to Victoria they went when they left Aberdeen. He was practically a stranger to them, and we heard later, when Auntie Maggie came across, that they had a dreadful time with him. They couldn't bring friends to the house because he invariably asked them if they were saved. All three of his children, grown up by then, were models of good behaviour, but they would hear him up in his room praying aloud for his godless family.

He stayed with us in Glasgow for a week and didn't bother us very much, though he was undoubtedly queer. Now that I think of it he had distinct resemblances to Auntie of Montgarrie, though she could be very attractive and he couldn't. He was much concerned, for instance, about Auntie Annie and Cameron and asked me if I thought they gave money to missions in China.

Surrounded

I hadn't given the matter any thought and didn't care either way. He had just two main topics, John Macneill (evangelist 1854–1933) and Aimée McPherson; the one he adored and the other he abhorred.

He was no more popular with his relatives in Aberdeen than he had ever been, in fact Auntie Isa always blames that visit for giving her rheumatoid arthritis. She says he ruined her nerves. For one thing he got up at 5.00am and prowled about the house till everybody was completely unnerved. When Auntie Isa came down at 7.00am he sat in the kitchen, mostly in silence. If she gave him a good plateful of porridge she was insulting him. If she gave him little, did she not remember that he was a grown man? The day he left they all went to the station with him and from there they went into Union Street and bought a new tea-set by way of celebration.

Some years later he came back. It was in 1932 just after your father died and we were preparing to leave Dingwall. He spent a day with us; I suspected that he meant to stay longer but didn't give him the chance. He said he had come because he wanted to know whether I was left with enough to live on. I gave him no encouragement to suppose that I was looking for anything from him, and though he was a wealthy man his sole contribution to the family resources was one shilling that he gave to you.

On his second visit he was firmly told that Isa was now crippled with rheumatism and that he must go into rooms. This didn't seem to offend him particularly, though he was offended that when he was at Mid Stocket he wasn't asked to say grace though he was older than John. His chief topic was the Virgin Birth. If somebody was mentioned to him he would say, 'Does he believe in the Virgin Birth?' or he would shake his head solemnly and say, 'He doesn't believe in the Virgin Birth,' till Auntie Jessie said to him, 'Look here, Charlie, we're not interested in the Virgin Birth and would be thankful if you would stop speaking about it.' When he left that time he didn't let them know by what train he was leaving, so they didn't have a chance to see him off. History doesn't say whether they had meant to buy a dinner-set.

A year or two later a cablegram came from Victoria to say that he was dead. No notice was put in the paper, and it transpired later that the aunts didn't mean to put in the notice or to wear mourning till they were sure he hadn't committed suicide. The news had got about, however, and the person who was taking the Gordon Mission service the following Sunday made touching reference to the death of Mr Charles Smith. It was an awkward situation. They found it difficult to face the surprised comments of all their friends. And they needn't have bothered. He had been knocked down by a motor car quite near his own house.

5

CAVE OF ADULLAM

(Before the first General Assembly of the Free Church of Scotland was concluded in 1843, a London firm occupied a nearby field in Edinburgh, pitched a specimen tent and proceeded to take orders for what were to be called 'clootie kirks'. The weather was kind in the year after the Disruption. For this the Heavenly Maker was given all the credit. When it was less than kind, and when storms levelled some tents to the ground, the blame went to the London manufacturer. For some time the Free Church head office provided a standard tent which held 500 and weighed about 5cwt. Weight mattered a lot if tents had to be transported often, sometimes hurriedly – when some land-owners refused them sites for worship. Some mission groups were to maintain or restore the use of such tents. One such group was the Gordon Mission, based in Aberdeen.)

The Gordon Mission was started in 1856 by a number of people who were sufficiently convinced of the need for it to build a hall, select evangelists and guarantee funds. These people formed themselves into a committee which managed the affairs of the Mission for many years. Three, perhaps more, Aberdeenshire lairds desiring to promote evangelism got together and financed and organised a mission to preach the Gospel in the country districts – in conjunction with the churches and to assist the churches' work. They were led by John Gordon, laird of Pitlurg and Parkhill (1827–82), after whom the Mission was named. Among others to be associated with it were Davidson of Inchmarlo, Banchory; and Bisset of Lessendrum, Huntly.

Dean Inge in his autobiography tells that he and his wife went to spend a short holiday with the Davidsons at Inchmarlo. After they had been there a day or two they heard to their surprise their host say at morning prayers, 'Give a safe journey to our dear guests who leave us today'. When I was a child I was accustomed to hear it said that Davidson's brother wasn't right in his head. He had a shed in which he made ships that he thought would fly.

The Gordon Mission was originally planned to work in connection with and under the direction of the ministers in country districts, to assist and feed the churches. But as the work in country districts and consequent donations also decreased there was a tendency to grudge 'food' for the churches. There was a Director and half a dozen evangelists, and while the Director remained to conduct services in the town the other evangelists held missions in churches in winter, and tents in summer. Gradually conditions changed. There was a quickening in the churches and more evangelical preaching so that outside evangelists were neither so necessary nor so welcome. At the same time there were changes within the Mission. As the original evangelists moved out, their places were taken by others who resented working under the direction of ministers and were inclined to set up in opposition. All this was very gradual, but today the Mission is a one-man affair and is practically a sect of Plymouth Brethren though they have never adopted that name.

By the time Uncle James became Director (1897) the staff was reduced to three or four and they were already inclined to sneer at churches and to claim that the Gospel was preached nowhere except in the Gordon Mission. In JA's time the Gordon Mission was increasingly anti-church.

One of the great themes in Gordon Mission teaching was The Lord's Second Coming – 'At such an hour as ye think not' etc. Two incidents come to mind. I remember hearing an evangelist speaking on this subject and he told as illustration a story about a man who was living in a hotel and paid his bill every night in case the Lord would come before morning and find him in debt. Another time I had been at a tent meeting with my mother, and Uncle James was preaching on the Second Coming and he said something about having nothing belonging to him but six feet of earth in Allenvale. On the way home my mother said, 'I do think it was very wrong of JA to speak like that. He owns two properties, but the grave in Allenvale is not his. His sisters bought it'.

They also took a special interest in the prophetic books of the Bible and often put names, e.g. the Kaiser, to figures mentioned in them. They weren't the only people who did that. Nurse

Grant once told me that her minister, a Baptist, had said that Hitler and Mussolini were mentioned in the Book of Daniel. No doubt their names were spelt differently.

The Gordon Mission had a number of tents and tent equipment – benches and an organ. I don't know what they did about transport but they did take their own stuff with them. The staff consisted of one of the GM evangelists and in the summer it was always augmented by young men from various missionary colleges in London who spent their holidays in this work. These were young men who were in training for the mission field and subsequently went abroad under the auspices of the London Missionary Society, the China Inland Mission, and the Regions Beyond Mission. There is also, or used to be, a college in Glasgow called the Bible Training Institute (BTI) from which recruits were drawn for the Gordon Mission and kindred missions. Many of the students became honoured and successful missionaries. Of the permanent evangelists in the GM, a fair number eventually entered the ministry, chiefly in the Baptist Church – their educational demands are not so great or didn't used to be. The last of them, Mr John W Currie, went into the UF Church in Glasgow and wears a minister's collar but I don't know whether he calls himself Rev.

They lodged in the country district where they had the tent – probably often got hospitality. They were both popular and helpful for a long time and many of the ministers welcomed them. The personal question no doubt always counted for a good deal – ministers could be difficult and so could evangelists, but the GM did a lot of good work. They had good financial backing from a number of county families, and from people who had enjoyed their services in country districts. They also took collections – had a collection box at the door.

Probably the 1914–18 war finished tent missions. All my childhood days, up to about 1902 or 1904, tent missions were part of my background. Uncle John spent all the summer months in the country – Banffshire, Aberdeenshire, Moray – having missions, staying perhaps a month in one place. There were at one time as many as four evangelists connected with the Gordon Mission who went to the country with tents. All over the North East they were a familiar and popular feature of country life. Eliza Grant, for example, remembers them well because of their visits to Keith, and when I went to Rothiemay in 1908 I was well received amongst the farming people as a niece of JA and John G Smith. I was only a few days in Rothiemay when my landlady, Mrs Donald, set a very small chicken on the dinner table. She said, 'I remember JA Smith the evangelist saying, "You've been cutting green corn," when we gave him a young chicken for his dinner. That was when we were at Redmyres in Marnoch. I don't suppose you'll know him.' 'Oh yes,' I said, 'he's my uncle.'

Uncle James told a story of when he had been conducting meetings in Portnockie. The morning he was leaving he went into a railway carriage whose sole occupant was a woman who evidently recognised him. She had expected an enquiry about her soul's health, for when he said, 'Good morning, it's a lovely day, isn't it?' she replied haughtily, 'That's between me and my God.'

In Aberdeen the Gordon Mission tent was set up in an open space – Footdee, Torry, Holland St and several summers in Belgrave Terrace. If it was within reasonable distance we were expected to attend – which we did more or less willingly till we grew up a bit and grudged the time. If too many nights passed without a Morrice being seen at the tent, Uncle James called to enquire into the family's health. We feared him far more than we feared God. At that time my mother held him up as the ultimate authority on morals and behaviour – 'I don't know what your Uncle James would think if he knew . . .'

The preaching in the tent meetings in the town was done by visiting evangelists from the South, some of them excellent and some not. I remember your Auntie Jessie having a dreadful night when she might have been about ten years old. She had been at a tent meeting in Holland Street and a Mr Clynes – a Cambridge graduate, what an absurd memory I have! – preached a hell-fire sermon. I hadn't been there but my mother had to come through in the middle of the night to deal with Jessie A's nightmare. Another story *re* that Mr Clynes – a Mr James Thomson, a Plymouth Brother on holiday from London, called on us. He was courting Auntie Annie at the time and making the acquaintance of her relatives. My mother mentioned Mr Clynes and he said, 'I don't approve of him. He forsook the light and left our meeting.' My mother's awesome, to me, reply was, 'You don't mean to say, Mr Thomson, that there is no light except in your small gathering.'

I don't know much about country tents and I should think they would have borrowed seats from the local hall. The town tent would have held several hundred people. There were plain wooden benches with backs, and boards along the ground in front of them to keep the feet off the grass. The tent was quite different from the 'tent', a small platform, that was common when Communion Services in the Highlands were held in the open air. There was one near the wood near the manse in Nethybridge, but only Gaelic services were held out of doors and not, I think, in my time. I don't remember seeing one.

There wouldn't ordinarily be any difficulty about the singing. If the evangelist or his assistant couldn't play and/or sing there would be some local person who could. Both my uncles were excellent singers. There was an organ – American harmonium – and the singing was mostly frequent and hearty and from Sankey's hymns or from a collection of evangelistic hymns – books given out at the door and collected at the door. Occasionally there might be an after-meeting or a testimony meeting but not often, and in the case of the meetings in country districts seldom if ever. The sermons and prayers were as varied as in any service, depending on the evangelist who was in charge. If a minister or well-known interested person was present he would be asked to take part in the service. The meetings were advertised in the local paper and there was a notice board at the tent. The percentage of men in any congregation was as high as in any church service, and children were neither encouraged specially nor discouraged.

The meetings could be demonstrative – people saying 'Praise the Lord' and suchlike – also counting of scalps, a proceeding your father abhorred at all times. The visiting evangelists, a succession of them, perhaps a month each, were often excellent preachers who came frequently to the tent or the GM Hall, and they preached as any minister would do on Old or New Testament subjects – no social or political bias that I can remember. There was a good deal of emphasis on Bible Reading. Some evangelists preached hell-fire and some were apt to denounce churches and ministers. My uncles and the Mission Committees discouraged anything excessive. They couldn't always prevent excesses. In the county districts the tent meetings were welcomed by the ministers who had evangelical tendencies, opposed by those who hadn't.

The eccentricities and oddities of which you have heard me speak were largely confined to the permanent section of the Gordon Mission and were easily enough explained by its very permanence. If you could imagine a Billy Graham mission, e.g., settling down in one place you could understand what would happen. My mother used to say that the GM was a Cave of Adullam (1 Samuel xxii 1,2). People whose minister didn't please them, who didn't get enough glory in their church, who had quarrelled with other office bearers, drifted to the GM, stayed for a while and wandered off elsewhere, often to the Plymouth Brethren. Gordon Mission converts were not encouraged to become church members.

I don't know when the changeover took place but for a good many years regular Communion services have been held, and the evangelist in charge even officiates at marriages. Presumably the couples are married at a Registry Office but I have seen marriages intimated as being 'by' the evangelist and recently there was a photo of one. My mother nearly had a seizure when she first heard of Uncle James in that capacity.

In Lyn Irvine's book *So Much Love, So Little Money* she says that her father distrusted and disliked the quick conversions of the tent preacher and his methods of achieving them. She also says that he mentions only the services of the Children's Special Service Mission on the beaches of Wales as influencing him in his decision to enter the ministry. He must have been lucky with his Children's Mission and unlucky with tent missions.

To my mind the fact that the evangelists had a natural facility was their undoing. I have no doubt that to begin with they were quite sincere, but it was easy to gather a fluctuating audience. Going from place to place they could have more people at a meeting than would normally be at the local church service, which gave them an inflated idea of their ability and popularity. They didn't feign learning, they despised it. One of them said to my brother Willie when he went to College, 'My mother is afraid you're getting too much learning for a minister'. Willie said, 'She believes in sanctified ignorance, does she?'

They believed in the literal truth of the Bible. Higher Criticism, Evolution, Science were all devices of the devil. They were like the Highland woman your father used to speak about. She found fault with her minister because he had suggested that the story of Jonah was an allegory. 'But,' he said to her, 'you don't believe, do you, that the whale actually swallowed Jonah?' 'Of course I do,' she said, 'I would believe that Jonah swallowed the whale if the Word of God said so.'

About the religious/scientific set-up in Scotland in my youth I think the Robertson Smith and Rainy stories pretty well sum it up. In our home, of course, there was a great deal of 'ooh-ah' talk between my mother and her brothers about Higher Criticism and Evolution. The fact that Robertson Smith was personally of interest did a good deal to take the edge off my mother's comments, but they were definitely anti Higher Criticism and Evolution and all that.

These evangelists preached Hell-fire and Judgment in the crudest terms. They also thought it necessary for salvation that one should be able to point to a day and an hour when conversion took place. If you could say 'I was converted on such and such a day' you were all right for time and eternity.

The only time I went to a meeting at the Gordon Mission after we came back to Aberdeen – you were with me, at least 25 years ago – a visiting evangelist was giving a lurid account of the Judgment Day. After depicting its horrors he said, 'Now you saved people, you're all right. There's no Judgment Day for you.' I was horrified, and still more so when I discovered that this was considered a wonderful sermon.

As we grew up we had all our interests within our own church. We went on special occasions to the Mission. But the Gordon Mission affected our home atmosphere very seriously. My mother was all for genuine evangelism but not too keen on the Gordon Mission. She sent us to represent the family on special occasions but went very rarely to it herself. We were, in fact, unpopular, because we were the only family in the connection who were spoken of, to quote my grandmother, as being 'kirky'. We are still unpopular and for much the same reason.

It was to Dr Leckie (Aberdeen Royal Mental Hospital doctor; at Kingseat Hospital) that my aunt Lizzie said her brother John had an 'abundant entrance' (2 Peter 1,11). I presume she meant that he had been the pattern of virtue to whom Peter promised it. The phrase is familiar enough to me and must, I think, have been the kind of boon that evangelicals craved in their public prayers. It would seem to me to savour of presumption. I doubt very much whether Lizzie or Jessie ever thought much about anything. Willie Smith, Glasgow, came round to Harcourt Road once after having been at 178. He said to me, 'I didn't know that there was anybody in the world like your Auntie Jessie. She actually believes that the world was made in six days of 24 hours each'. AJ and I were wondering when Isa died whether Jessie had any questions in her mind or if she pictured Isa walking streets of gold. I remember when John Morrison was killed in France your father who was in France at the time and had been hoping to arrange a meeting with him, wrote me, 'I wonder under what circumstances John and I will meet again.'

In *The Singing Days* I came across in a description of a little girl playing with her dolls this sentence: 'She reprimanded them with a smile of the insolent who offers two fingers to an inferior.' I read this to your Auntie Jessie and said, 'Whom do you think of?' and she replied, 'Uncle James'. I hadn't been aware that this was a recognised gesture – the only person I ever saw doing it was Uncle James. There were people who spoke of it as offensive. I then told Helen that I'd been amused to find a reference to the two-finger handshake in *Victorian Miniature* which is delighting me. Speaking of an occasion when the Vicar had words with the Squire, it says, 'Andrew held out his hand. The Squire hesitated whether to take it and then protruded two fingers'. Yes, the two first fingers were held out by James and I can assure you it was a most offensive gesture.

Uncle James and Uncle John were both money-minded but in different ways. James wasn't mean but crafty. He was grandiose but managed to get into people's wills, not only my grandmother's and Auntie of Montgarrie's but several rather worthwhile ones. Having never had more than £120 a year of salary, he left £8,000 which 40 years ago was a large sum of money. My mother used to say that his name should have been Jacob. John was openly and shamelessly mean. He boasted that he never paid for a holiday and never went for a game of golf unless invited and paid for. He used to go on holiday with the Camerons – Auntie Annie – and one year he went to Switzerland with Lizzie and Jessie. I heard Lizzie, after she had become forgetful enough to 'tell' things, remind Jessie that John borrowed money for that trip from her and never paid it back. After he died Auntie Jeannie said to me, 'To my certain knowledge his salary was £90 a year till he succeeded James and then for his last three years it was £120 – and he left £3,000'. In both cases their estates were a complete shock. My guess is that if they had been put to it they would have said that the Lord had wonderfully provided.

I have an uneasy suspicion that I have unfairly biased my family against hyper-evangelism and for that reason take the liberty now of hoping that you will deal sympathetically with Tom Allan (then well known as an ardent C of S evangelical minister in Glasgow. CM took part in the late 1950s in a BBC Scotland television Press Conference featuring Tom Allan). My relatives are and were, some of them, samples of the worst results of the 'be saved and do as you like' preaching. On the other hand what might they have been like without their evangelical background? – keeping in mind their domineering and money-grasping proclivities.

Your Father and I

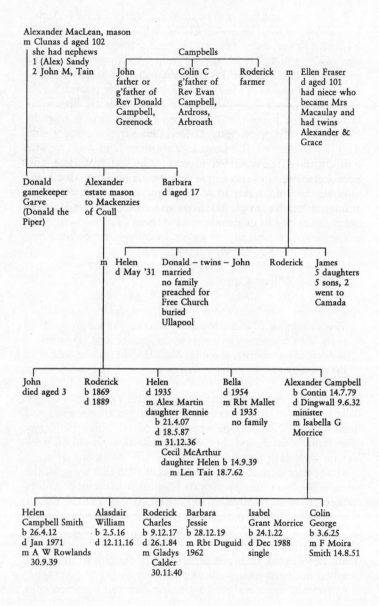

Alexander MacLean, mason
m Clunas d aged 102
  she had nephews
  1 (Alex) Sandy
  2 John M, Tain

Campbells

John
father or
g'father of
Rev Donald
Campbell,
Greenock

Colin C
g'father of
Rev Evan
Campbell,
Ardross,
Arbroath

Roderick
farmer

m Ellen Fraser
d aged 101
had niece who
became Mrs
Macaulay and
had twins
Alexander &
Grace

Donald
gamekeeper
Garve
(Donald the
Piper)

Alexander
estate mason
to Mackenzies
of Coull

Barbara
d aged 17

m Helen
d May '31

Donald – twins – John
married
no family
preached for
Free Church
buried
Ullapool

Roderick

James
5 daughters
5 sons, 2
went to
Camada

John
died aged 3

Roderick
b 1869
d 1889

Helen
d 1935
m Alex Martin
daughter Rennie
b 21.4.07
d 18.5.87
m 31.12.36
Cecil McArthur
daughter Helen b 14.9.39
m Len Tait 18.7.62

Bella
d 1954
m Rbt Mallet
d 1935
no family

Alexander Campbell
b Contin 14.7.79
d Dingwall 9.6.32
minister
m Isabella G
Morrice

Helen
Campbell Smith
b 26.4.12
d Jan 1971
m A W Rowlands
30.9.39

Alasdair
William
b 2.5.16
d 12.11.16

Roderick
Charles
b 9.12.17
d 26.1.84
m Gladys
Calder
30.11.40

Barbara
Jessie
b 28.12.19
m Rbt Duguid
1962

Isabel
Grant Morrice
b 24.1.22
d Dec 1988
single

Colin
George
b 3.6.25
m F Moira
Smith 14.8.51

66

6

The Sun Always Shone

Achilty 22 Dec 1868

It is contracted and agreed between Alexander McLean and
Ellen Campbell both residing in Achilty in this parish of Contin
to enter the holy bonds of Matrimony and do each bind and
oblidge themselves to get Maried with in the space of eight days
the party failing to pay the sum of 40 Scots £s.

Signed Alex McLean
Ellen Campbell
witness Wiliam Chisolm
John Ross

(transcribed from handwritten original, in spelling of original.
The spelling of Maclean/McLean/ MacLean varied over the
years and from person to person in the family, until my father
decided, in his twenties, to opt for MacLean, the spelling used in
the remainder of this text.)

I paid my first visit to Contin in June of 1910. Your father's sister
Bella had visited us in Aberdeen on several occasions, and I had
spent a day at Nethybridge when Alick Martin, his wife Helen,
your father's sister, and their daughter Rennie, an infant, were
staying with your father on holiday.

Motor cars were still so uncommon in 1910 that we went the
three miles from Strathpeffer to Contin in a Victoria. Oddly
enough I have no recollection of my first sight of a motor car, or
of my first ride in one, though I do remember seeing a man riding
in Whitehall Place, Aberdeen, on a penny farthing bicycle.
Motors were all open and we were nearly blown to pieces in
them. People took their pleasures in great discomfort and went
swathed in motor-caps, veils and scarves.

A Victoria, however, was a comfortable and dignified conveyance, and all the visitors who went in summer to the Strathpeffer Spa drove about in Victorias. Your father had a story about Donnie Munro and himself. They decided that they must get money somewhere and that it would be a good idea to gather and arrange wild flowers and sell them to passing visitors. Accordingly when they saw an old lady with her maid being driven leisurely up the road to the Strath they approached and held out a large bunch of flowers. The lady smiled kindly but shook her head. Infuriated at this failure of their first effort, your father threw the bunch after the carriage, hit the old lady on the back of her head and knocked her bonnet – no hats for the aged in those days – over her face. They heard the maid laugh but did not linger. Nothing short of imprisonment awaited them and they didn't dare to show their faces on the roadside for several days.

I have never been much attached to places but can understand how some people feel about them because of my feelings for Contin and Cromarty. The sun seems always to have shone in Contin. All the people about there seemed gentler and kindlier than Aberdeenshire folk, and I can truly say that no-one of your father's family ever spoke an unkind word to me. I was immediately one of them. Their affection for your father, and for me because of him, never ceased to surprise, accustomed as I was to the constant adverse criticisms of my own relations. Many years later, when Uncle Bertie died, Bella said to me, 'He had a smile on his face as if he had just seen Alick.' There was this great difference, too, between the Contin folk and my relatives, there was no urgency about them. They took life easy and interfered with nobody. The lovely voices and accents of the Contin people were a continual joy to me. They were all bilingual and though they spoke English in general, your grandfather always said grace and conducted worship in Gaelic.

Your grandfather, Alexander MacLean, was born and lived all his life in Contin. His father, also Alexander MacLean, lived near Loch Achilty and was, I think, a mason. Your father never saw him but used to visit his grandmother in the cottage which was still standing when I went to Contin. Her name had been Clunas but he had no particular recollection of her. What he did remember was that a visit to her filled him with terror because he had to pass the cottage of a certain Widow Kemp who was said to have the evil eye and to be able to make cows stop giving milk, and to have other strange powers. It was believed that as night came on she turned herself into a hare. Even people like your grandparents who didn't believe she was a witch wouldn't have run any risks.

There were three in the family, your grandfather, a brother Donald and a sister Barbara. The sister died when she was seventeen. I never saw Donald MacLean though he was still alive when I went to Contin – in fact we were in Glasgow when he died.

The two brothers had very little in common. Your grandfather was clever, industrious and serious-minded. Donald was a gamekeeper and lived by himself at Garve. He was known all over the Highlands as Donald the Piper because he won the prizes for piping at all the Highland games. He was at the famous Wet Review in Edinburgh when Queen Victoria and the Prince Consort reviewed the Scottish Regiments, and had a daft story that when he was playing the pipes before the Queen he slipped and fell. She said, 'Rise, MacLean' and he replied, 'Thank you, Ma Queen.' Evidently his sense of humour was outsize. When your father was particularly annoyed with his sister Bella he would say she was like her Uncle Donald MacLean. She wouldn't have said so. One morning when old Uncle Donald was seated at his breakfast, a remark was made about a neighbouring couple who hadn't been very long married. 'Is there an issue?' – pronounced 'eesue' – said Donald. When he rose and went out Bella said, 'Coarse beast, what a word!' When I have seen Sybil Thorndike on television I have thought she is very like your Auntie Bella.

When Donald died the Stirlings to whom he was gamekeeper were abroad and somebody who was in charge wrote your father for permission to open the MacLean burying ground in Contin churchyard. He also suggested that he would be glad to know who was going to pay the funeral expenses. Your father felt obliged to say that he would, but remarked to me that it was hard lines, since Donald had never in his life given him a sixpence.

Your other great-grandfather was Roderick Campbell, a farmer at Achilty. He had two brothers – John, the father of Rev Donald Campbell, and Colin, grandfather of Rev Evan

Campbell. I never heard anything of Roderick Campbell except that he was highly respected. His wife was a Fraser from the Black Isle. I think they must both have come from there because they are buried in Killearnan Churchyard.

Your Campbell great-grandmother was a woman of strong character spoken of with awe by all her grandchildren. She must have held the record for one thing – she had four children in one year, twins in January and twins in December. The January twins died, but the December ones lived to be very old men.

Your grandmother, Helen Campbell, was the only daughter and she had four brothers, Roderick, Donald, John and James. James built a wing to his house in Inverness when his mother was too old to live alone. She lived to be 101 and your MacLean great-grandmother to be 102. Occasionally she lived for a few weeks at Contin and your grandmother took the chance to go for a day to Dingwall. When that happened Granny Campbell contrived to thrash not only all the MacLeans but all the neighbours' children as well.

Your grandmother was something of an enigma to me. She was kindness itself, always indicated that she approved of me, but she wasn't a talker. By the time I knew her she had grown far too stout, which perhaps accounted for her lack of energy, though your father had always found the lack of energy irritating. She undoubtedly had second sight. There were a number of stories in proof of that but unfortunately I remember the details of only one. When they were newly married your grandfather and she occupied one of the lodges at Coull House. He was estate mason to the Mackenzies of Coull, as well as having, either then or later, a contractor's business of his own. One night when the eldest child was an infant she got up to get a drink for him, and looking out of the window saw the laird's funeral pass up the avenue. She noticed it in every particular and identified the various carriages and their occupants. The laird and his family were in London and nothing had been heard of his illness or death. It was in the late 1860s and there were few postal or transport facilities in the Highlands, but the laird's funeral had set off from London that night and in three days' time the funeral procession passed up the avenue exactly as she had described it.

There were five children in the family, John, Roderick, Helen,

Bella and Alexander. John died at the age of three of scarlet fever whilst he was still the only child. Roderick died when he was 20 of pneumonia. He was studying law and was apprenticed to a solicitor in Dingwall. His death was a blow from which the others never fully recovered. Your father was only ten at the time but his big brother had been his hero and he often spoke of him. Your grandfather had been a fine fiddler but he never again touched his fiddle. Your grandfather was clever – hasty, cross and very affectionate. His daughter Helen was his favourite. Bella and he struck sparks.

When your father was a child the cottage in which he had been born was enlarged: the walls were heightened and bedrooms put in upstairs. Previous to that there had been a bed in the kitchen and his only recollection of it was connected with his first remembered humiliation. It was the custom in the district for a dressmaker to stay in the house, perhaps once or twice a year, and do all the necessary sewing, make dresses for mother and daughters and shirts for the male members of the household. The time would vary, naturally, according to circumstances, but he thought she stayed a week or a fortnight. There was so much activity in the house, everybody sewing from morning till night under the expert direction of the dressmaker, that he was left to play around till he dropped asleep and was then undressed and put into the kitchen bed. He remembered vividly the fearful scene he made when he awoke one morning and discovered that this woman had also slept in the kitchen bed during her whole stay in the house. He must have been very young at the time, because it was while the workmen were in the house that his next tragedy took place. He took a keen interest in all their activities and one of the men said to him, 'Man, you're far too inquisitive.' He didn't know what 'inquisitive' meant but had no doubt about it being an insult.

The Contin neighbours were so much part of the picture that the story can't go on without them. There were four Contin cottages and they had been occupied for many years by the same families – Campbells, MacLeans, MacKays and Munros. I never saw the MacKays, two brothers, and a sister who acted towards the other three families much as Uncle James did in our family set-up. The MacKays had occupied the next cottage to the MacLeans all their young days. They were regarded as the ultimate authorities on correct conduct. William MacKay, a retired teacher, stood no nonsense, and the sister Annie was *censor morum* to the whole district. The other brother was negligible. They had died before my time, being succeeded in the cottage by Frasers. Annie, the last of them, had recently died and was a subject of much conversation. Bella MacLean and Mary Munro had each helped themselves to their favourite piece of furniture, Bella a table and Mary a chair, in the face of anguished protests from their parents. They used to go into gales of laughter at the thought of what Annie MacKay would have said. 'What would Annie MacKay think?' was still a familiar question after I came on the scene.

The Campbells were the estate gardeners, and a second generation of them occupied the cottage by the time I knew it. Kenneth Campbell had married a south country woman who wasn't really of the race of Joseph, but an excellent neighbour and very helpful to your grandmother. They had a son Alickie, an only child, who was the same age as Rennie Martin and the bane of her life when she was at Contin. Your sister Helen used to play with Alickie Campbell, who was four years older, and with Connie McDonald from Tain who spent her summers with her aunt, another not-so-close neighbour. They spent hours making a concoction, chiefly water and earth, which they called Beastie Beer Wine and having parties with it. There was a great fuss one day because they all went along the road to play near an old sawmill. They found aniseed growing there and ate it. Helen remembers the fuss but doesn't remember what it looked like, just that she thinks she ate leaves. None of them suffered any harm except Alicky Campbell who probably ate more than all the rest put together. His mother came in to find out what they had been doing because Alicky was very ill – sick I suppose – at any rate she said he was 'cracking with wind' and they were disgusted. Not that Contin people couldn't be vulgar – they could! – but Mrs Campbell was a Glasgow woman and her vulgarity was considered different. She had come to Contin one summer as housemaid with the McGregors who took Contin Farm for their summer holidays. Kennie Campbell married her – a sign of his supposed simplicity. He suffered by contrast with his brother Allan who was a Chief Detective in Glasgow.

The Sun Always Shone

The Munros were the exact contemporaries of the MacLeans and were as nearly of the same family as possible. Donnie Munro and your father were born in the same week and were inseparable. Mr Munro was the forester and the finest type of Highlander. He was an old man when I knew him, quite bald and white bearded, but in his youth he had been very handsome and had raven black hair. He was a fine singer and precentor in the Free Church. His hair early began to turn white to the great distress of his wife. She sent for a much-advertised hairdye and with great difficulty persuaded him to put it on one night when he was going to bed. Next morning his hair was all on the pillow. On Sunday with commendable courage he took his place as usual in the precentor's chair. After church his friends were all asking each other who was the bald man who was precenting?

Your father was sent with a note one day to a woman who lived near Loch Achilty. When he returned there was a houseful of visitors. His mother said, 'Well, did you see so and so?' 'Yes,' said he, 'and what's she but a hoor anyway?' A dreadful silence fell upon the company. He hadn't a notion why he said that or where he heard the word, but it happened to be true.

Your father would have gone to school in 1885 or '86 probably, but his parents had gone to the same school and had the same headmaster. The school was, still is, situated near the road which goes from Muir of Ord past Garve to the West Coast, and it was a one-teacher school. Mr McGlashan, the headmaster, was highly respected as an efficient if stern dominie. No complaints about punishment were listened to by parents who had been his pupils. If Mr McG punished you, you needed to be punished. One or two stories make one doubt the wisdom of that attitude.

The day Jimmie Munro went to school for the first time he was playing with the other boys round the school door waiting for it to open. The excited noise they were making was too much for Mr McG. He came out and gave the strap to all of them, including Jimmy, so that he had been chastised before he had even entered the school. One day your Auntie Helen was going home from school walking as any child will with one foot in the ditch and the other on the road. She was wearing the then fashionable white cotton stockings. Mrs McG passed along, and

73

next morning Helen was taken out to the floor and punished before the day's work began, for dirtying her stockings on the way home from school.

One of Mr McG's crazes was to insist that the pen should be held with two fingers straight along the back. If a child was failing to manage that he would say, 'Are your hands cold?' If the answer was 'Yes,' he said, 'I'll warm them for you,' if 'No,' then the strap was given because orders were not being obeyed. Friday afternoons brought a wonderful relaxation. Every pupil was allowed to read a passage of his or her own choice out of the reading book. There was one girl who never failed to get up and start with great zest, 'Wasps are papermakers'.

Twice a year Mr McG became human; he collected the school fees! He called at the homes of the pupils, got his money – it would be interesting to know how much – gave a penny to each pupil present, and then spent a social evening with the household.

Shortly after we were married your father and I were in Edinburgh and called on Mr McGlashan and a daughter who kept house for him in his retirement. I remember him as the typical old dominie, no moustache but jutting white whiskers and unexpectedly benevolent air. Incidentally it was the first time I had seen toast made on the grill of a gas cooker. It was also the first time I heard anybody call your father Sandy.

Soon after your father was ordained at Nethybridge I went to spend a week-end with the Campbells in Inverness. It was a happy hospitable home which we visited frequently for many years, but what impressed me most then was the difference between their Sunday and ours. The Campbells were Free Presbyterians, a sect I had never before heard of though they were numerous in the Highlands. Helen had warned me not to sing hymns in the house. 'Pa doesn't mind songs,' she said, 'but he won't allow hymns.' That seemed to me then, and still does, quite irrational.

On Sunday morning we went to the FP Church and the minister preached for an hour and five minutes on 'The lamp of the wicked shall be put out'. I wasn't there in the evening but was told that he continued the same sermon for another hour. After dinner the whole household was gathered round the dining-room table and catechised. It was quite a household too: five daughters, three sons – two of the sons were already in Canada – Jimmie Campbell a cousin from Glasgow, Uncle John Campbell from Contin, Mr and Mrs Campbell and myself. Uncle James Campbell went round the table asking questions out of the Shorter Catechism beginning at the first and pursuing to the last. I created a sensation by being word perfect in every answer. Having tried Welfare of Youth exams at Sunday School and Donaldson exams as a pupil-teacher, the Shorter Catechism was as familiar to me as the alphabet. What did astonish me was that none of them knew the answers. Mr Campbell asked a question, if it wasn't answered he passed it to the next who might make a guess at it. Mrs Campbell sat at the table but if she heard a question she took no notice. That a dozen people could and did sit round a table being asked questions and unashamed and unrebuked fail to answer them was something new in my experience. I still find it difficult to understand though I now know that it's a kind of indifference and incompetence characteristic of many Highlanders.

The rest of the day everybody spent as they thought fit so long as they stayed indoors and didn't sing hymns. The Free Presbyterians who were our neighbours in Dingwall did no work at all on Sundays, didn't even wash a dish. They didn't read newspapers, weekday or Sunday, didn't take delivery of milk on Sundays and some of them kept all their blinds drawn for the day. So far as I know they didn't differ from the other churches in Scotland on any point of doctrine. They seceded from the Free Church in 1893 because of the Free Church Declaratory Act of 1892 which gave more freedom to ministers with regard to their ordination vows.

All ten of the Campbells, five sons and five daughters, married Free Presbyterians. I noticed in a Sunday paper some time ago that a daughter of the youngest daughter and John Grant, an Inverness banker, was in trouble with hospital authorities because, being Matron of a Home for Children, she refused to allow fresh milk to be delivered to it on a Sunday.

The Wee Frees and Free Presbyterians sing only metrical Psalms and Paraphrases in church. Some of them are not too keen on Paraphrases. The only time we stood for prayers was when we were visiting Wee Free and Free Presbyterian services.

We never stood for prayers in Rutherford Church or at Mission services.

A Sunday in Contin was peace itself. Your father cycled to Strathpeffer to the United Free Church – Mr Johnstone – and I went, if possible, with whoever else was available, to the Island, the Parish Church – Mr MacLean. If Donald Campbell, your father's uncle, was preaching in the Hall, somebody went there. But there was no fuss, no questioning or organising. In Contin the rest of the day was like any other day. The pressure in the Campbell home in Inverness was quite different.

Mrs Munro and your grandmother went one day to have tea with a friend two miles from Contin. When they arrived and knocked on the door they got no answer, and repeated knocks brought nobody. They couldn't understand the situation and crept cautiously to the windows and looked in. Their hostess was kneeling at a chair obviously engaged in prayer. They were surprised; after all she had invited them. She was a nice woman but they hadn't known she was so devout. They withdrew to a bench in the garden to consider whether they should return home or wait events. By and by the cottage door opened and the minister came out. He had been making a pastoral visit, but was not visible from the window.

Mr Munro came to see us in Nethybridge and stayed with us for a few days and so great was your father's regard for him that he relaxed his teetotal principles so far as to make todddy for him every evening at bed-time.

There had been a tent mission, not Gordon Mission, in Contin just before I first visited there – so far as I know the only one. It had been a great success and whereas hymns were never sung in church they had been enthusiastically welcomed in the tent, and small paper-covered hymnbooks sold. Mary Munro was as thrilled with them as teenagers are now with pop songs. She would say to your father and Bella and me, 'What about coming this evening for a ceilidh?' and we would drink tea and chat and sing – songs and tent hymns. Old Munro who had been a precentor in the Free Kirk all his grown-up life and wouldn't have imperilled his soul by singing a hymn in church sang as heartily as the rest. Mary's great favourite was one that I have managed to remember partly:

The Sun Always Shone

I have a Friend, a precious Friend
    Oh how He loves me
He says His love will never end
    Oh how He loves me

He walks with me along life's road . . .
He carries every heavy load . . .

Why He should come I cannot tell . . .
In my poor sinful heart to dwell
    Oh how He loves me.

It had one of those nostalgic tunes and I used to sing it to Helen – to all of you, I suppose – but one night when I was singing to her she said, 'Why has that friend got no name?'

Mary Munro's ceilidhs are long past – in the incredibly carefree days before the First War – and I am the only one of that company that is left. Your father never had anything to do with tent missions. Not that he disapproved of them.

We went every summer to Contin till after we had gone to Glasgow when the distance was too great and the fares too expensive for so many of us. Usually Bella and Helen and Rennie were there too. Bella, in fact, didn't leave home till she went to work at munitions after 1914.

There was a yearly blanket washing which was quite an occasion. Your father and grandfather started early in the morning, built a fire beside the river at the bottom of the garden, put a huge iron pot on it, and filled it with water from the river. Every blanket in the house was brought out and wooden tubs gathered round the fire. The menfolk kept the fire going and the pot filled and the women – Mary Munro joined the company but your grandmother didn't – tramped the blankets, exactly like pictures of a Highland blanket washing that you sometimes see on post cards. They were all dried and back on the beds before night. Your aunts would never have thought blankets were clean if they hadn't been tramped. They tramped theirs in the bath when they lived in Glasgow.

Rennie being several years older than Helen didn't always see eye to eye with her, though on the whole they got on very well. They played endlessly in a building called the workroom at the top of the garden. This place contained hats and dresses that had collected over the years. Your grandmother didn't believe in throwing out anything – 'It might come in useful,' she would say. Every time her daughters went home they suggested clearing out the workroom but she wouldn't hear of it, and then one day she went along the road to see somebody and forgot to lock the door. When she returned there wasn't a rag in the workroom. Mrs Campbell next door had met a tinker on the road and wondered where she had got the load of clothes that was on her cart.

The workroom also contained all the picture postcards that had ever come to the house. They were a great entertainment but one day they were all the cause of a great row. Somehow one of them reminded Rennie of my brother Willie for whom she entertained a romantic passion. I don't remember whether she had ever seen him but her claim on him was too much for Helen. There were high words and Rennie retired to her bedroom for the rest of the day. She did this every time she was displeased. One day she put all the green peas out of her broth round the edge of her plate so as to savour them when everything else was finished. She was asked to fetch something from another room and when she came back Helen had eaten all the peas. Rennie still speaks of this with some bitterness. I don't suppose she starved in her isolation; her mother no doubt carried food to her.

Uncle Donald Campbell was often at Contin. After his wife died and he had retired he lived alone in his house in Inverness but sometimes he stayed in Contin with your grandmother for weeks at a time. He must have been about 70 when I first saw him but he was so vigorous that rather than go round by Dingwall when he went from Inverness to Contin he walked the seven miles from Muir of Ord station. He ate brose every morning and sometimes at other times as well. One of his theories was that people should eat only the food that grows in their own country because Providence had so arranged. I don't know what Donald Campbell did for a living except that he spent his working life in Ullapool. When I knew him he was by way of being retired but worked for his brother James Campbell in Inverness who was, like your grandfather, a building contractor. Donald and his twin brother John appeared to have tried various jobs. John was a tram driver in Glasgow. But they were most probably stonemasons.

Like your grandparents, Donald belonged to the Free Church and had not gone into the United Free Church (The UF Church was formed in 1900 by the Union between the United Presbyterian Church and the Free Church of Scotland). There was no narrow-mindedness in that; the United Presbyterian Church had been practically unknown in the Highlands and most of the Highland people saw no need to join a church of whose existence they were not aware. The Parish Church at Contin was one of the oldest churches in Scotland and stood on an island at the junction of two rivers but it was very poorly attended. The Free Church was at Jamestown two miles away and had at that time no regular minister. Donald Campbell spent his Sundays preaching in Gaelic all over Ross and Sutherland. I don't think he was paid by the Free Church but he was fully employed by it. When he preached in Contin Hall it was crowded out whilst there weren't more than a dozen people in the Parish Church.

He was a remarkable man, short and dark, with tremendous breadth and depth of chest, and a peculiar detachment from ordinary life. When he sat down to breakfast he usually said, 'Well this is the day our Maker has sent us,' and he was started for the day. He had a deep booming voice and Bella used to imitate him striding about with his hands in the tops of his trousers saying, 'We are all going on a journey'. He once stayed with us for a week in Cromarty. He was a dear old man but he did speak Scripturally all the time. One evening Miss Fleming was there and he discoursed to the two of us all evening about Solomon. His English was a bit odd. He would say, 'I heard Dr Kennedy preach to a large ad-u-ance on the text . . .' and then the sermon would follow.

When he was 88 years old and still in good health he wrote to your grandmother who was then in Glasgow, 'Come home to Contin. I expect to be going Home in the autumn and I want to see you.' She stayed in Contin for the summer and Donald came to see her. He walked the seven miles as usual, stayed a few weeks, and back again to Inverness. He took to bed but had no complaint of illness and for no apparent reason slipped out of life. He was buried in Ullapool where he had spent all his working life. Your father said he had never seen anything like his funeral. As it crossed Ross-shire groups of people joined it every few miles on the way.

Another interesting person was a cousin of your grandfather, another Alexander MacLean, always known as Sandy Clunas. Your father lived with him from Monday to Friday in term time whilst he attended Dingwall Academy. Sandy owned a double cottage on the High Street. One end of it he occupied himself and in the other Mr Duff lived with his family – the same Mr Duff who as an old man was one of the elders in Castle Street Church, Dingwall. Sandy was a bachelor and was much attached to your father. We were in Cromarty when he died. As your father was getting ready to go to the funeral he said to me, 'I had forgotten, but Sandy used to say he was leaving his house to me. I wonder what I would do with it if I got it'. As they were walking to the cemetery Mr Duff said, 'I believe you're my landlord now. Sandy told me he had made a will leaving everything to you.' There was dinner for the people from a distance but no word of a will, and when your father rose to leave, Sandy's brother, John MacLean, from Tain, came to the door with him and taking a walking stick out of the stand handed it to him saying, 'I'm sure Sandy would have liked you to have this keepsake of him.' He never heard or enquired whether there had been a will but when he took the walking stick as he set off for a walk he sometimes said 'I'll take my house with me'.

Isabella's family, the Morrices: Isabella, Helen, Charlie, Jessie, William, Willie.

Isabella's father and mother.

Isabella and Jessie.

Four generations: Isabella, Helen, Helen, Isabella.

Alexander MacLean, with sisters Helen and Bella, and parents.

Alexander MacLean's parents.

Alexander MacLean, c.1905.

Alexander MacLean's mother at Contin cottage door.

Alexander MacLean (top right) at Carloway School.

Alexander MacLean (right),
army chaplain.

Isabella MacLean's brother,
Charlie, in uniform.

Alexander MacLean, Isabella MacLean and (centre)
Helen MacLean.

Mrs Hope (see p.139), Barbara, Colin, Isabel.

Colin MacLean, with parents.

The funeral of Alexander MacLean in 1932. Roderick stands in the foreground, with uncles alongside.

7

IN HIS SERVICE

Rutherford United Free Church
Aberdeen
29th October 1906

Dear Mr McLean

Your resignation of the Office of Missionary* was laid before the Kirk-Session at a meeting held on 21st October.

The Session, having no alternative, accepted the resignation with regret, and resolved to place on record their high respect and esteem for you, and their warm appreciation of the excellent service you have rendered to the Mission and the Congregation during the three years you have been Missionary.

The earnest, faithful and enthusiastic manner in which you have carried on the work of the Mission, and the large measure of success which has attended your efforts, have been most satisfactory and gratifying to the Session.

Your appearances in the Pulpit of Rutherford Church have been always welcome, and the services you conducted there were much appreciated by the Congregation.

That your future steps may be ordered of the Lord; that you may be long spared to labour in His Service; and that His blessing may rest in abundant measure upon you, and upon all your work for Him, is the earnest desire of the entire Session.

I am,
Yours very truly,
William Herd,
Session Clerk.

(* In the late nineteenth century some better-off congregations opened Mission Halla in poorer areas: these were usually managed by elders from the parent church, led by a Missionary – often a young probationer minister. In this case the Mission Hall was only a short distance from the parish church.)

While your father was a student at Aberdeen University he taught for three summers – March or April to September – one year in Kylestrome, West Sutherland, and two years in Carloway, Lewis. In fact he taught for a whole year in Carloway, taking a year's break from College for financial reasons. Very few students took the summer term. While in Carloway he had a small house and your Auntie Helen kept house for him. Miss Rainy, sister of Principal Rainy, ran the Ladies' Highland Association of the Free Church of Scotland which paid students to teach in the Highlands in the summer. Kylestrome, for example, had no school except in summer. I remember a meeting of the Ladies' Association in the Divinity Hall in Glasgow at which your father moved the adoption of the report. He told the meeting that he had been one of Miss Rainy's men and spent a year in Carloway at a salary of £40 which was so ample for himself and his housekeeper that he had money in hand when he left it. Rev James Barr, later an MP, rose and said he had one question to ask, 'What salary did Mr MacLean pay his housekeeper ?' We have a photo of your father with his pupils at Kylestrone – Mrs Stewart, Lentran, who gave you the electric clock as a wedding present, was one of them.

Your father was a fine precentor. He filled that office all the time he was at the Divinity Hall and when we were at Dingwall he precented for the Annual Conference at Strathpeffer – in the Gaelic – giving out the line. Dr Hetherington of Blantyre was thrilled with it, said it was the nearest thing he had ever heard to the native African singing, which he considered the finest music.

I remember Dr Robert Rainy (1826–1906, Free Church leader, Principal of New College, architect of 1900 Union, played prominent role in FC unrest over William Robertson Smith's writings) preaching in Rutherford Church to a tremendous congregation and afterwards to the Bible Class – the first time Jessie and I were at it. We probably didn't go regularly for several years after that but we were ardent meeting-goers. Your

82

father, then in his first year in Arts, was there and often referred to that Sunday's services. He also had a genuine admiration for Rainy but by the time I knew your father William Robertson Smith was accepted. Your father would never, I think, have been so personally aware of the WRS conflict as my family were. His parents, though deeply religious, were not so articulate as my relatives unfortunately were.

In 1906, your father's last year in the Divinity Hall, the Quatercentenary Celebrations were held at the University and King Edward and Queen Alexandra came to the opening of the new buildings at Marischal College (The quatercentenary should have been celebrated in 1895: the celebration was postponed until 1906). His cousin Helen Campbell came from Inverness for the occasion and stayed with us. She and I sat on the roof of the Divinity College in Alford Place, along with others, to see the King and Queen drive past. We had an excellent view. Edward was like a stout hearty farmer, and Alexandra as beautiful as a statue and as lifeless. There was a procession of graduates in the afternoon and the famous Strathcona Banquet in the evening. The photo of your father in gown and trencher was taken that day. He had been teaching in Lewis at the time of his Arts graduation and was capped in absentia. He went to the banquet, found it very boring and was amongst those who left early. Champagne flowed like water, unwary graduates had no idea of its potency, and it was said that scores of them spent the night prostrate beneath the tables.

Your father never remembered any dates but one – no birthdays and not his wedding day but November 17, 1905, the date of our engagement, and if you can solve that puzzle it's more than I could. It used to amuse me. We were married on 27 April 1910 in Rutherford Church. None of our parents were there. My father was too ill; he only managed to sit up for the tea-party which was in our house. The reception in the Palace Hotel was cancelled when he grew ill. The Contin parents had long stopped leaving home. I never met them till June, but already knew Bella and Helen and Alick Martin and had stayed for a weekend with the Campbells in Inverness. In Contin it was considered very 'simple' for a young man to bring his fiancée home. Jockan Matheson did it and was poorly thought of.

I was once at Haddo House and only once. Your father and I

spent the first week of our married life at Cairnorrie with the Macdonalds and they were within driving distance of Haddo House. The gamekeeper there was a Contin man and he and his wife invited us to dinner and to see over the House, Lord Aberdeen etc being away from home. I remember the dining room curtains in Haddo House, 53 years ago, their colour, pattern, price etc. I also remember that we got chicken soup for our dinner with far too much rice in it.

Until you asked about it I don't think it ever occurred to me that your father never so far as I remember gave any explanation of why he went in for the ministry. Probably it was just taken for granted – it very commonly was in religious Scottish homes. The fact that his brother Roderick, who was a law apprentice in Dingwall, had decided to go in for the ministry if he recovered from his illness may have had something to do with it. Your father didn't at any time indulge in the kind of talk which was common amongst my mother's folk. My father didn't either. If my father had ever said about anybody, 'He's a converted man' or, 'She's not a saved woman,' I would have been seriously alarmed. Your father was a thoroughly enlightened and fully educated man who didn't get het-up about other people's views. He didn't seem to think they mattered so very much if people were honest. I rather think that if you manage to read his sermons you will agree that his message was positive and had little to do with railing at other people.

Just once your father told me of an outstanding experience. He was staying overnight in John Macdonald's home at Cairnorrie – that puts the date at some time after he had started divinity. He was very depressed and uncertain about himself. At family worship JM either read the 59th chapter of Isaiah or quoted in his prayer, 'Behold the Lord's hand is not shortened that it cannot save, neither is His ear heavy that it cannot hear', and from that moment he harboured no doubts.

His attitude towards the ministry is difficult to explain. On the one hand he was absolutely dedicated to it, and on the other he had very little patience with ministers in general. He could be very sarcastic about the 'important' kind of minister who was jealous of his social position etc, and even more so about the 'ideal' minister's wife, but his intimate friends were nearly all ministers and they were of the race of Joseph. There were

84

aspects of his devotion to his calling that I personally found trying; in fact I felt compelled at times to protest. He saw no reason why his wife and family shouldn't be equally devoted. No plan of ours was proof against an interruption from somebody who was of no interest to us at all except that they belonged to his church. And money which couldn't be spared for family use was liable to be given freely to a stranger. On the question of a minister – I fancy that it applies only to ministers – expecting that his family will support every generous and quixotic gesture of his – it's a subject on which I have rather mixed feelings. Winifred Peck in her book *Through Eastern Windows* represents her father, Bishop of Coventry and father of Ronald Knox, to have been an exaggerated example of this, and Pearl Buck in a biography of her father, a missionary in China, has the same picture.

About a couple of months ago I read a *Times* obituary paragraph about a man – name forgotten – who had been on the staff of *The Times*. It said that he had been married to the writer, Leonora Eyles, who died a good many years ago. The name rang a bell. In our early days in Cromarty, Leonora Eyles had a series of articles in *The Quiver* on, I think, Husbands in the Bible. One of them was about Moses and Tipporah and she gave Moses the same kind of write-up. I must have been peeved about something at the time because it gave me quite a new slant on the situation and kept me from making it a personal issue.

Your father said he had always admired Mr Stewart, who was our minister in Rutherford Church, but never more so than when he heard that when his affairs were wound up there was only £11 left. To be sure, he had educated a sizeable family when there was no Carnegie fund. Your father's attitude towards ministers and their finances could be very aggravating but at least it was consistent with all that the ministry stands for. Fortunately my reading of miscellaneous articles and books had made me aware that this is by no means an uncommon trait in the dedicated type of person, but as Helen and Roddie grew up they showed signs of resentment and rebellion. I could give you a large number of instances but I fancy you know most of them already.

He was quite reasonable about his demands from his family if a quiet protest was made. I may say here and now that I never knew him to give way to temper. He could be cross and irritable if things weren't done to please him but only in a minor kind of way. The expectation of cooperation from his family was an instinctive kind of thing with him. He expected them to feel exactly as he did, that they were so much at one with him that they would put the congregation first. I think perhaps this story which can't be new to you gives a really good idea of what I mean. Before we went to Dingwall Miss Morrison gave me an evening dress of hers – a very pretty shade of red velvet. I made it into a party dress for Helen when she went to College – high neck, long sleeves, all very decorous. Our first Christmas in Dingwall the choir was having a party and they invited Helen to it. She had only the one suitable dress and wore it. Next day your father said to me, 'Do you think it was in good taste that Helen should have been the best dressed girl at that party?' and went on to say that there should never be any idea that the minister's family was in any way superior or privileged. I made all the obvious protests – Helen knew nothing of it at the time – and said that I believed his psychology to be at fault. The choir girls would have felt insulted if she had gone in every-day dress. They would know perfectly well that she must have some kind of a party dress and would say, 'Anything is supposed to be good enough for us'. I have since thought that it evidently never occurred to him that she was the only girl there who was being expensively educated and was likely to occupy a better position than any of them, but they weren't supposed to mind that. I needn't elaborate the situation further. What worried me was the inevitability of revolt on the part of the family – it was the expected thing in ministers' families. But he wasn't of the stiff-necked order who would refuse to see reason.

His attitude to the temperance question never really altered. As an individual he had no self-indulgences, as a minister he held that he had a special responsibility for the weaker brother. He did however say that in his preaching he wouldn't if he had to begin over again make abstention from alcohol an end in itself. It should be part of temperance which is one of the fruits of the Spirit. He also observed that most temperance lecturers and rabid TTs were notably intemperate in their other habits. In practice he was wonderfully helpful and often successful with alcoholics, even if he never quite succeeded with Willie M, though poor Willie was the most ardent admirer that any man ever had.

Your father wasn't an ardent politician though he was Liberal. I've no doubt he kept himself well informed but he didn't take the same interest for example as my father did. He had a theory which I know he once put into practice that if you know one candidate who is a man of outstanding integrity and common sense you should vote for him. I remember that he voted for a Maryhill barber, a Socialist, for that reason and that Kenneth Cameron was shocked at him.

I don't know whether his theological views altered with time – not that I know of. He was an independent type, not given to following this person or that. You ask if he was tolerant. He wasn't intolerant. I would say that he was tolerant about people's views, to use a word much abused by my relatives. 'What strange views he holds!' was a favourite and infuriating remark of theirs. About conduct he was a perfectionist and intolerant. 'If a thing is to be done it should be well done' was a frequent saying of his. Having had perfect health until the last four years of his life he had no understanding of incapacity to work long hours, for instance. He said himself later that if he had had any idea of what it feels like to be ill he would have had more sympathy.

Your father and mine were the two most satisfactory people I ever met. That is to say, that nothing would have made me believe that either of them would have departed from the truth by a hair's-breadth, or taken a mean advantage of anybody – quite the reverse – or grudged anybody's success, but it has to be borne in mind that whilst your father died at the age of 52, mine was 52 when I was born. Your father had a very keen sense of humour and appreciation of absurdities, and wasn't at all touchy. In fact he had little patience with people who were over-sensitive. I never managed to cure him of practical jokes, though I particularly hate them myself. He never appeared to have any difficulty about getting on with Sessions and Deacons' Courts and the like. In fact his personality was so commanding and so pleasing that only impertinence would have made it possible for anybody to be difficult, and he was well able to deal with that. He had no personal axes to grind.

I have a big bundle of your father's sermons. A mouse got into the desk once in Harcourt Road and I was compelled to throw out some mutilated paper. Also I gave your Uncle Willie some sets of sermons – the Minor Prophets and the Ten Commandments for instance – but I would never have dreamt of throwing them out. They are written in a synoptic style of his own. He never read his sermons, but his extempore style of preaching didn't mean that he just spoke at large. He memorised his sermons thoroughly. Your father had a beautiful voice – and so had Donald Campbell and Evan Campbell. I have always thought the family voice somewhat flat and like my own.

In common with most Highland students of his day, your father had never read a novel till he was 25 years old. By the time I met him he was already a graduate and must have read all that was appointed to be read for a degree pass in English. There was not in his time, nor in mine, home reading for school.

There were very few books in Contin – William Law, Thomas Boston, *Life and Sermons of Dr Kennedy of Dingwall*, Sunday School Prizes and the like. The Contin folk weren't readers and neither were their neighbours. *The Inverness Courier*, *The Ross-shire Journal*, and during the fortnight of the Assembly *The Scotsman*. Such books as they had must have been thoroughly read, for your father had in his youth turned *Boston's Fourfold State* into verse – how much of it I don't know, but it was a hefty bundle of foolscap he found when we were clearing up the Contin house. I must have told you already that the copy of Tennyson's poems that we have here is the prize he got at Dingwall Academy for the best poem on Queen Victoria's Diamond Jubilee.

The Contin folk maybe didn't read but they were in no doubt about what other people should not read. Novels were dangerous lies and no conscientious person would read one. I gave your father on loan the first novel he read – *The Scarlet Woman* by Joseph Hocking, a story about Catholics, and he sat up all night to read it. *The Scarlet Pimpernel* got the same treatment. Then he discovered George MacDonald. He was reading *David Elginbrod* in Contin when his Uncle Roderick Campbell – Glasgow Wee Free – was on holiday. There had been a very heated discussion which didn't influence your father in the least. He respected his uncles as decent Christian men but had no sympathy with the narrowness of their religious views. His general reading was all designed to be useful for sermon-making and illustrating. That did not prevent it from being an unfailing joy to him.

What I say here about your father's reading has no bearing whatsoever on his professional reading. In Divinity he held the Eadie Prize for Greek, and Professor Cameron thought highly of him as a Hebrew scholar. He was much in demand as a preacher in Gaelic but never willingly took Gaelic services away from home. The reason for this was that his Gaelic was colloquial. Easter Ross Gaelic was poor Gaelic and he was very conscious of having little knowledge of the grammar. In fact he went to classes in Dingwall (1930–32) to learn it.

From the time of our marriage till 1914 – outbreak of war, after which we seldom sat down to a meal by ourselves – we finished almost every meal with a reading. He ate very slowly, I ate quickly: he loved to be read to and I loved to read, so nothing could have been more satisfactory. We read steadily through the English classics – Scott, Dickens, Eliot, the Brontes, Thackeray, in addition to such up-to-date biographies and novels as came to hand. I particularly remember Wells' *Mr Polly*.

When Helen was old enough to be read to, her father enjoyed her books as much as she did – *Christie's Old Organ*, *Jessica's First Prayer*, *A Peep Behind the Scenes* - and in later days the Anne books. *Alice in Wonderland* was as new to him as it was to her, and he knew it practically by heart, could quote it to great effect. I remember that in his first letter from France he said that when he was crossing the Channel he was saying to himself, 'The further off from England the nearer 'tis to France, So turn not pale beloved snail but come and join the dance'.

Alexander Reid has an article (18.1.59) about Annie S Swan in this month's *Scotland's Magazine*. I don't care for it at all – it has the cynicism and the silliness of all that Lallans set-up, and it has the usual kick at Kailyard stories. He says Annie Swan's stories were fairy tales etc. The fact is that her stories were much nearer life as I have known it in a number of country places than anything, most things, I read nowadays. She wrote about nice people, but why not? Why go past the rose-garden so as to sit in the midden? I must start writing letters to the papers.

It was commonly supposed that every Friday morning all the housewives, when the family had departed for work and school, sat with their feet on the fender and read the new instalment of an Annie Swan story in the *People's Friend*. I know it was the case with a great many and if they met afterwards on the stair or in the backgreen they would say, 'Well, what do you think of so and so today?' We all loved *Beside the Bonnie Brier Bush* and all that set. I still do, and without feeling any need to apologise. I have personally known so many of the type depicted in the Kailyard kind of book that nothing would make me cry them down. And I am not without experience in human nature – Rothiemay, Nethy, Cromarty, Contin, Glasgow, Dingwall – and an insatiable interest in what people do and why they do it. I think it was many years before I realised with dismay that they were despised and even given a horrid name like the Kailyard School. Robertson Nicoll wasn't a bad sort. I would be inclined to look on him as the person who popularised reading in ordinary homes as nobody else ever did.

I wonder what I would think of Robertson Nicoll if I could come to him fresh, so to speak. He was so much part of our background – literary, ecclesiastical, family – that it's difficult to say. I never saw him, neither I fancy did my mother except once, and that was when he spoke at the opening of the North Church in Aberdeen. Your father was there too, came back early from his holidays on purpose (1905?). They were bitterly disappointed that his voice was extremely ugly – thin and harsh and his appearance unimpressive.

Though our reading was slowed down by the war which filled our house with visitors and lodgers, and altered to some extent by the demands of the family, it never stopped. In the later years when there was no servant, especially when we were in Dingwall, I read to your father after dinner whilst he did the accumulated dish-washing. I don't remember very particularly what we were reading at that time – upstairs with Roddie in bed we read the Pooh Books, lent to us by the Turnbulls (Mr Turnbull was headmaster of Dingwall Academy). It was not unusual for me to be so tired that my voice died away and I fell asleep. Since Roddie spent both our winters in Dingwall in bed, and my sister Jessie was laid up on my hands for months it wasn't too surprising.

The wave of crime fiction hadn't broken on the country in the 1920s but Charlie Chan books were popular at that time. Your father was much interested in them, but more, I think, for their Chinese proverbs than because of crime detection. He didn't care for comic books, though – perhaps because – his sense of humour was so keen. He had a peculiar aversion to Wodehouse, though he had only attempted one or two of his books. He didn't find them funny and the people were all so inferior.

I am sending, for your interest, an old copy of *In Memoriam*. It was Auntie Jessie Smith's before it was mine and copiously annotated by us both. I have no doubt all the comments were dictated by our teachers. Tennyson was the prophet of The Larger Hope and very unpopular therefore with people like the Elder Brother of the Prodigal.

8

REDOUBTABLE CHARACTERS

I have been lucky with congenial neighbours – Miss Fleming in Cromarty, Miss Bain in Glasgow, and Mrs Bisset in Aberdeen. I could miscall my husband and family to them and fear no aftermath. It's a great help, especially when you realise afterwards how grossly unfair you have been.

Except for the Malcolms and Miss Fleming, Mr and Mrs Scott were our most intimate friends in Cromarty as they were our nearest neighbours. (Mr Scott was the C of S parish minister. Alexander MacLean became UF minister in Cromarty in 1912, having been UF minister in Nethybridge since 1908.) The Parish Manse was in the town, but it was an enormous and inconvenient house. Mrs Scott owned the property which adjoined the UF Manse and had an attractive house, Rosenberg. They preferred to live there. They let the Manse to naval officers and their families from April to October.

Rev Walter Scott was an Edinburgh man and his first charge had been at Kilmany where his first wife died. Mrs Scott belonged to an old Cromarty family. Her father was Colonel Brydon, famous as the last man of Kandahar. When I was young there was a popular calendar which pictured him riding into Afghanistan wounded and on a jaded horse. She was born in India and was sent home to Cromarty with her nurse when she was an infant, at the outbreak of the Mutiny.

There had never been anything but the barest civilities between the two manses until our time and the reason for their taking so kindly to us was shockingly simple. The first Sunday of July was Communion Sunday in Cromarty and your father intimated his arrangements a few Sundays before. He got an agitated letter from Mr Scott the next day pointing out that the first Sunday in July was Communion Sunday unless it so happened that the preceding Thursday was in June. Thursday was Fast Day and if the two churches didn't agree as to dates there was confusion among the shopkeepers. That was all perfectly reasonable and your father called on Mr Scott and explained that he had acted in ignorance, never having been told otherwise and that he had no intention whatever of acting contrary to custom. From that day Mr Scott looked on him as a son; he consulted him on all their mutual interests and even invited him to share his dog-cart when they went to their respective Presbytery meetings at Fortrose. The sight of them setting out together never ceased to astonish their parishioners.

Mr and Mrs Scott were both people of ample private means and lived in old-fashioned style, dined late and dressed for dinner and had a sufficient staff of servants indoors and out. They had an old-fashioned factotum called John Campbell who was beadle in church, acted as coachman, and superintended garden boys. Mrs Scott had a story about him that one day she said she wanted a fowl killed for dinner. 'Well,' said John, 'we'll hae that white ane. She's full sister to the cock,' When they had interesting visitors they either invited us to lunch with them or brought them over to call.

Mrs Scott came over to see me most forenoons about 10 o'clock – very inconvenient for me but she was incapable of realising that. Sometimes she had a note of the things she meant to speak to me about. She was very interesting to listen to, having been abroad a good deal and having met interesting people. When she was of an age to go to school, instead of having a governess she went along with the girls of her own age and class to France or Germany. In September the young ladies from the Highlands converged on Cromarty and waited in the Inn at the harbour for the boat that would take them to London en route for their various schools. They returned in early summer.

Mr Scott had a son and a daughter of his first marriage. The son went to Canada – forced to leave home, according to gossip, by the unkindness of his stepmother. There did seem to be some justification for the story because he came across with the Canadians during the war and called at Rosenberg. In the evening Mr Scott took him down to the YMCA and asked the superintendent to put him up for the night. 'You see,' he said, 'it's a stepmother my son has and not a mother.' The daughter, Mrs Romanes, came occasionally and we were invited to meet her. The atmosphere was coldly polite between her and her stepmother. Her two sons were young boys then; they are both Catholic priests now. Her joining the Catholic Church was a great grief to her father.

Our Mrs Scott had one son, Francis, exactly the same age as myself. We saw very little of him. He was a handsome, pleasant fellow with no vices that I ever heard of, but he never managed to earn a living. He was educated privately along with the Middletons, and they sent him at great expense to Oxford where he didn't take a degree. They put him into a fruit farm in Hampshire and in a few years he went bankrupt. Then they tried him with a sheep farm on the Black Isle and again he failed. When his mother died he settled down in Rosenberg on what was left of her money and spent his few remaining years working about the garden.

Now (1961) Rosenberg is a guesthouse for part of the year. Helen has just spent two nights in Cromarty and she was assigned to Rosenberg, next door to her birthplace, because the hotel was full. She is keen that I should go to it sometime but the idea doesn't appeal to me. I'm sure I would be unbearably homesick. I still can't think without tears of the day I left Cromarty. Leaving Alasdair broke my heart. I hoped for a boy in 1917, when Roddie was due, to soften the blow about Alasdair. To replace him would not have been possible.

Mr and Mrs Scott were people of the most impeccable personal behaviour but they were conservative and Auld Kirk to a degree. They took no cognisance of or interest in such things as evangelical preaching, temperance reform or schemes for the education and betterment of the masses. They would have been kind to the poor of their congregation but very definitely 'the poor'. I never heard Mr Scott preach and I imagine he would have been pretty dull, but he was a courteous gentleman and highly respected in the district. Mrs Scott wasn't well liked. She did her congregational visiting in the forenoon, lifted the lids off people's pans to see what they were having for dinner, and gave much unwanted advice. Dr GF Barbour, of Bonskeid, had been at Rosenberg for tea one afternoon and told us afterwards that Mrs Scott had given him a most amusing account of how the Salvation Army had tried to start a branch in Cromarty. He paused for a minute and then said in his hesitant way, 'One felt that it wasn't entirely sympathetic.'

To illustrate the difference in outlook between us I must tell you what she said to me on one of her forenoon visits. She was very pleased and excited because a young sailor whose ship was in the Firth had called the previous afternoon. His father had been a Coastguard in Cromarty and attended the Parish Church and had told the boy that if ever his ship was in the Firth he must call on Mr and Mrs Scott. She told me about him and his people and then said, 'I told him that the next time he is here he must come and have tea with the maids.'

In spite of her peculiarities she was a good friend to me. She was highly educated and a great reader and kept me supplied with books that wouldn't otherwise have been available. Without interfering in any way she took the greatest interest in all our concerns and was always the first visitor to see a new baby. She frequently gave me presents though she had an embarrassing way of referring to them: 'Dear Mrs MacLean, I do hope you are finding the dressing gown I gave you useful'. She gave me a boudoir cap, a wonderful affair of lace and blue ribbons. I wore it once – the day I was expecting her to come and see the new Barbara – deceitful? It was afterwards made into a baby's bonnet. Even after we went to Glasgow she sent me presents at Christmas.

I had a casual meeting with Ethel Smythe at a Red Cross fete in Cromarty in the summer of 1913 or 1914. Mrs Scott who was a terrific snob, which makes her attachment to me inexplicable, was very impressive about Ethel Smythe. I knew nothing at all about her and she seemed a large, loud, fearsome-looking woman. She was with Lady Maud Warrender, who sang The Three Fishers. Lady M W was the wife of Sir Charles W who was in the Firth that summer with the Home Fleet of which he was Admiral. She was also the daughter of the famous Earl of Shaftesbury and for that reason far more interesting to me than Ethel Smythe.

Your father and I were guests at the first wedding in Cromarty of the mother of the Rev Simon Phipps: he is often in the news as being a friend of Princess Margaret. His mother married a son of the Earl of Ancaster, Peter Willoughby, who went down in the Monmouth in 1914 or 1915. It gives me great pleasure to

Your Father and I

remember some of the clothes I had then. When May Ross was married in Cromarty to Peter Willoughby there were nine countesses present and the Cromarty people said I was the best-dressed person there. How's that for a proud boast! A plain silver grey silk dress with a black hat with black ostrich feathers and one white ostrich feather round the back – 1913, so I was quite young.

Mr Scott christened both Roddie and Barbara in the house, Roddie because your father was leaving for France(1918), and Barbara because we were going to Glasgow(1920). He had had a slight shock before he christened Barbara and got confused. He said the funeral prayer instead of the baptismal one; Mrs Scott got very agitated and stopped him when he said, 'We thank Thee for the days and the years that Thou hast spared her'. He died in the spring of 1925. He had left instructions that your father was to be asked to conduct his funeral service: your father went through from Glasgow to Kilmany to do so.

Mr Scott once brought Dr James Cooper (Professor of Ecclesiastical History, Glasgow, and C of S Moderator 1917) to call on us in Cromarty and I thought he was a pet. He was spoken of in Aberdeen, in our set, as being unorthodox. Your father was out and I entertained them for quite a long time. Dr Cooper and I were buddies and he said he loved to hear me say Aberdeen as only an Aberdonian can say it.

General, later Sir, Walter Ross was the Cromarty laird. He was a hero of the Boer War, had half of his jaw shot away and an artificial one in its place. His first wife had been a lady of high degree and they had one daughter who is the mother of that Rev Simon Phipps. His second wife was the daughter of a brewer, wealthy and handsome but not quite acceptable to people like Mrs Scott. When she first came to Cromarty she tried to get the children to curtsey to her, but they wouldn't. The Rosses didn't belong to our church but came often in the evenings and brought their visitors. They were very pleasant and friendly but we didn't know them well, and I mention them only to show how changed society is. They owned all the farms from Cromarty to near Rosemarkie. Gradually these have been sold and now (1961) there is nothing left but Cromarty House, the Home Farm and a few of the houses in the town.

The second Mrs Ross had two sons and three daughters. They

were insufficiently educated – privately – and were not fit for careers. The daughters married. One of them is a widow and runs a club in Edinburgh. Geordie, the laird, was in the Army but was cashiered for going out with a horse without leave and breaking its knees. They took him back of course during the Second World War. He now runs the place as a strawberry farm, sends strawberries by plane to America, and works harder than any of his employees.

When we went to Cromarty in 1912 there were still plenty of odd characters in it – odd but not too odd. Most of the ones we knew need no more than a passing word. Kennie Duff was an oldish man, or seemed so to me. If he had ever worked at anything I never heard of it; he seemed just to stand about on the pier or at street corners. He told your father once that he was a good man because he always kept his Bible beneath his pillow; probably he couldn't read. The only interesting thing about him was that Tom Mackay, a nice kindly young fellow, was never allowed to forget that he killed Kennie Duff. Kennie, who lived alone in a garret, fell ill and Tommy visited him and took various comforts to him. He was distressed, however, that the invalid was deplorably dirty, hadn't evidently been washed for years, so he determined to put matters right. He gathered all that was necessary, heated water, and washed Kennie from head to foot. Next morning Kennie died. The doctor said there was no doubt that the shock killed him.

Blind Benjie was a poor little creature with a straggly beard who went about playing a fiddle. He was almost totally blind and was probably defective in a harmless, well-meaning kind of way. He lived with a sister whom your father didn't like – he wondered whether she was kind to him. But Benjie brought in a good deal of money which sailors gave him when the Fleet was in. He played quite well by ear, and when your father visited at the house Benjie started to play hymns whenever he recognised his voice. When the war finished he was put into the poorhouse at Fortrose. Katie McKeddie who lived nearby told us that the sister never went to see him though Benjie lived in daily expectation of her coming. When he wasn't carrying his fiddle he went about clapping his hands first in front of him and then at his back. In the poorhouse he went about doing this and saying, 'I've washed my face and combed my hair and she's no come yet'. I'm glad to say that he didn't survive more than a few months of exile.

Dannie Screech, whose real name was Donald Sutherland, was a very different type. He looked like a wild man of the woods – broad, dark and bearded, and was harmless but a nuisance. He had a house, or perhaps only a room, near the church and maintained himself after a fashion doing odd jobs of labouring. By the time we knew him he lived alone, but he had been married and had a son and a daughter. In his younger days he had set his affections on a woman as far from normal as himself and asked Mr Scott to marry them. This Mr Scott steadfastly refused to do and Dannie went around telling his tale of woe to everybody. A few youths got hold of him one night and told him that if he and his girl-friend went to the parish church on Sunday forenoon and stood up after the benediction and declared themselves man and wife they would be legally married. They were well coached and on Sunday, accompanied by the youths, they sat at the front of the church and said their piece. Mr Scott thereupon agreed to marry them. The son and daughter were both more defective than either of their parents and were still in Inverness Asylum when we left Cromarty.

Dannie was put out of his house and had to go to Fortrose Poorhouse, but he ran away from there and your father let him live in a shed at the top of our garden till some other arrangement could be made. He worked about the garden sometimes and got most of his meals handed out to him but I was very glad when he left. Ranald Macdonald came from Dingwall to take a Fast Day service at that time and when he was taking a walk round the garden he said to Dannie, 'Mr MacLean has his garden in very good order'. 'Aye,' said Dannie, 'it's my poor back that knows it!' Ranald was furious and said, 'What on earth makes you keep a rascal like that about the place? Dolly Middleton said to me once, 'It's very good of Mr MacLean to bother with Dannie Screech, but do you like having him about the place?' 'No,' I said, 'but I'm so thankful he didn't suggest putting him in the spare bedroom that I'm putting up with it.'

Speaking of spare bedrooms reminds me of a curious visitor we had in the summer of 1914. A man arrived at the door one evening and asked if we would give him hospitality for the night. He handed in a card inscribed 'John Hunter, Man of God'. For once your father showed little enthusiasm about the Christian duty of hospitality but the man couldn't be turned from the door. It so happened that we were going the following day to Kenneth Maclennan's induction at Fortrose. Your father was to preach the sermon, and we had promised to go directly after breakfast to Avoch and have lunch there with Ewen MacLean. So John Hunter agreed to go on his way as soon as he had had breakfast. He was a nondescript kind of man and inoffensive enough, but we didn't take to him. When he retired to rest we felt that there was no guarantee that we wouldn't all be murdered in our beds and your father even suggested turning the key in his bedroom door – not that he would ever have done it – when the Man of God opened his door and put out his shoes.

Ewen MacLean was aghast when he heard that he was likely to have this man on his hands. John Hunter had told us that he had mapped out his itinerary, and Avoch was included. He was going round the Highlands – he was an Irishman – and preaching to such congregations as he could gather in the open air. Poor Ewen had a tartar of a housekeeper and didn't dare suggest that he might bring anybody in for a cup of tea. We were specially favoured because she had a nephew in Nethybridge. We heard later that John Hunter duly arrived. Ewen explained to him that he couldn't invite him to stay but gave him money to pay for his lodgings in the hotel. That availed him nothing. JH preached in the village that evening and said their minister wasn't a saved man, and the next time the housekeeper lifted the study carpet she found a paper inscribed 'To the minister of Avoch. Prepare to meet thy God. John Hunter, Man of God'.

Another strange character who was in Cromarty but not of it was a man Smith, a plasterer from Buckie. He came for some reason or other during the war and was never called anything but Contract, pronounced Coantract, because he said he went to the Parish Church in the morning and the UF at night so as to get any contracts that might be going. He pursued a chatty but inoffensive way until 1918 when a number of men were called up and their wives and families left defenceless. Then Contract, perhaps with the intention of being a help and defence, began to visit them frequently. He never visited me except in an afternoon when it was easy to get rid of him. Sometimes there would be a long interval of peace when he was away on 'contracts' but towards the end of 1919 the visits became a menace. Mrs Malcolm and Mrs Gaskill were the chief victims. He would arrive in the early evening, seat himself in the husband's chair and sit there through babies' baths and children's lessons and leave about 10.0 o'clock. They were compelled to lock their doors and refuse to answer for friend or foe.

Your father was by this time under call to Glasgow and was very busy, at meetings or visiting, and was often out in the evening. Barbara was due to arrive in December, we were quite isolated and I was nervous of being alone. One stormy November night a rose bush kept knocking on the sitting room window and I fancied it was Contract and panicked. By the time your father came in I was reduced to incoherency and fit only for bed. I had the most frightful nightmare. The front-door bell rang and I went to the door. It was Contract and he slipped in past me and went between the open door and the wall. I tried to seize him and push him out but when I took hold of him he seemed to have something made of leather under his suit and my hands kept slipping. My screams wakened your father and here I was raised up in bed scrabbling wildly at the sheet. He was fearfully alarmed and had great difficulty in assuring me that I was safe in bed and Contract nowhere near, but I was never left alone again. If he had to go out he saw to it that somebody came to keep me company.

Contract returned to Buckie – so we learnt later – but not till he had robbed Roderick Matheson's shop. The Mathesons lived above the shop and Mrs M's sister, Bertha Urquhart, worked in the shop and lived with them. One morning when it was beginning to get light she heard a noise, got up and looked out and saw Contract going down the street. She thought nothing of it till the shop was opened and the till found to be empty. There was no possibility of fixing the theft on him in spite of the fact that his two sisters who lived with him spent money very freely through the town for some time afterwards.

One man in Cromarty, John Macleod, when asked to pay his debts – which he never did – used to say, 'Don't worry about that – the Lord will provide'.

But there were worthy and intelligent folk too who could be amusing. The shopkeepers and tradesmen had very little competition, some of them none at all, and could be rude with impunity. Mr Johnstone, the chemist, was an elderly man who had four sons, two of them doctors, one the local doctor, one a chemist and one a minister. He was so domineering that people were often afraid to ask for things. Mrs Middleton, Davidston, once asked for soothing lozenges because she was apt to cough in church. He refused to give them to her: 'When I have a cough,' he said, 'I stay at home and don't annoy my neighbours.' When we broke one of Helen's feeding bottles, our servant Annie Leslie refused to go and buy another because he berated her soundly for having broken the last one. I hadn't been down to Cromarty for some time after we went there, and the first time I saw Mr Johnstone I said that I had come to pay for our newspapers. He looked at me in silence for a minute, went to look up the amount of our debt and looked at me again over his spectacles. Then when he took the money he said, 'Are you the minister's wife?' 'Yes,' I said. Another long look, and he said 'Oh!! Fancy!!'.

Gilmore, the plumber, was another independent character. Mrs Scott once said to me, 'I can't imagine why it is that we can hardly induce Gilmore to come and do anything for us, but if *you* send for him he responds immediately. And he belongs to our church, not yours'. I thought I could have enlightened her. Gilmore had to be asked, not ordered. I saw a note Mrs Scott was sending to the butcher and it said, 'Mrs Scott requests the butcher to send . . .' Murdo Grant, the banker, said Gilmore must have a magnetic personality because Mr Grant's nephew never left him for a minute when he was in the house. We felt that Helen felt the same magnetic influence. She was thoroughly interested in him. One day she said, 'Gilmore's trousers were torn. I saw his cossi-caissies (combinations)'. A thoughtful silence and then, 'What if he hadn't had cossi-caissies?'. Captain Pelham-Burns who had rented the Grahams' house met Gilmore and said to him in his lah-di-dah way, 'Oh, Gilmore! I wish you would come and attend to our bathroom taps. They won't stop running'. 'Weel,' he said 'they can rin for me!'.

Mary MacLean – called Mary Hoochtie because she kept goats – was a quiet, decent little body who lived with a very old mother. She must have been stupid because one day she left her mother, who was so ancient and done that she couldn't sit up for any length of time, in a chair before the fire. The poor old thing slipped out of the chair and her feet went into the old-fashioned open fire. David Taylor happened to be nearby and smelt leather burning so he went in and found her. She wasn't really much burned though her boots were smouldering, but she was badly shocked and died. However, it was a good many years later that Mary Hoochtie became famous. In 1920 or 21 a Swedish ship was wrecked outside the Sutors. It drifted and was towed into the Firth and abandoned on the shore about a mile beyond Cromarty. The local folk helped themselves to anything useful that was washed in. Mrs Roderick Matheson was in the Cottage Hospital and had an unobstructed view of the shore road. One afternoon she noticed Mary Hoochtie coming along with a good-sized box-like parcel under her arm. It appeared to be very heavy for she stopped often and hitched up the parcel with difficulty. Fortunately she wasn't the only one who noticed her. Such security officers as were still about the place were warned and went without delay to her house and found her setting a box of TNT to dry before the fire. There was enough explosive, they said, to have blown everything and everybody in Cromarty sky-high. Mary had noticed the TNT but thought it was some fancy kind of tea.

Of all the strange people I ever met Mrs Archibald was the strangest. We had been only a few days or weeks in Cromarty when your father was told that a Miss Ellison had died and her sister Mrs Archibald wished him to call and arrange about the funeral. Accordingly he called and when he came home he said it was a queer-like set-up and he had had a bit of a shock. Mrs A received him in a business-like way, he didn't find her prepossessing, and she ushered him straight upstairs to a room where Miss Ellison lay in her coffin dressed in bright blue. He said 'fully dressed' and I have always pictured her as wearing a hat but I can't vouch for that. We hadn't at that time heard of American Gardens of Rest and Mortuary Parlours, nor indeed for many years after, and this departure from custom was shattering. After the funeral Mrs A presented your father with a sovereign, the only time he was ever paid for conducting a funeral service. The Ellison burying ground was surrounded by a high iron railing and in addition to having a huge monument in it was heavily concreted from corner to corner. Every Sunday afternoon when weather permitted, Mrs Archibald carried a folding chair to the churchyard, unlocked the gate in the iron railing and sat in the concrete enclosure reading the news-papers.

The Cromarty people feared and avoided her. She belonged there originally, the house she lived in had belonged to her parents and was called Ellison House. Nobody seemed to know anything about Mr Archibald, but they had lived in America and made a lot of money – by disputable means if stories could be believed. The only passport to Mrs A's regard was to make a fuss about dogs. She always had a great number of them, eight or nine, and was delighted to look after any sick dogs that were handed over to her. She quarrelled with Mr Grant, the banker, and because his dog took fits and he got it put away transferred her account to Mr Ross's bank. When one of her dogs died she got David Taylor to make a coffin for it and he had to attend the funeral and listen to her reading the funeral service over the grave. There were a great many of them buried in her garden. David Taylor was the local carpenter, Session Clerk in our church and a somewhat narrow-minded man, so his services to Mrs A's dogs were always a matter of wonder.

Without having any repulsive features she was most unpre-possessing in appearance, and she dressed atrociously. In all the years we were in Cromarty she never appeared to have any change of raiment. On Sundays she wore an ancient, black dolman-like affair and a fearsome black hat; on week-days a navy-blue dress, longish grey coat with a black band on the left arm and a blue knitted cap with a tassle on the top. She attended church regularly but I never heard of her expressing interest in anything religious. She sat in the seat behind the Coopers and Walter Cooper declares that one Sunday when he was restless she leant forward and gave him two resounding slaps on the side of his head.

Mrs Malcolm met Mrs Archibald one day and, strange to say, Mrs A had a lady, evidently a visitor, with her. She stopped and introduced them. 'This,' she said, 'is Mrs Malcolm, a nice plain woman, but you should see her husband! A pompous little gentleman!'.

The Cromarty congregation was so far in advance of the Nethybridge one that they had an organ but it was played at the evening service only. Mr Armstrong, one of the teachers in the school, was precentor at the morning service, Mr Armstrong died in the summer of 1914 and the Session agreed that the organ should now be played at both services. It so happened, but only Mrs Archibald noticed it, that we had gone on holiday before the change in the morning service took place. Your father was going along the High Street the day after our return when he met Mrs A. He said, 'Good Morning' and offered to shake hands but she put her hand behind her back and said she wouldn't shake hands with a coward. He couldn't imagine what she was speaking about, but she soon enlightened him. It was a very cowardly thing, she said, for him to absent himself from his church the first morning the organ was played.

She didn't absent herself from church, however, but left as soon as the sermon was finished so that she would be spared something of the organ. She didn't believe in the Sustentation Fund, now called Maintenance of the Ministry Fund, but in order to show that she was willing to help in the support of her own minister she gave us a 20 gallon cask of paraffin every winter. I don't know whether it was because of cowardice or because he thought it infra dig but your father utterly refused to go and thank her for it and that unpleasant duty fell to me. She was civil enough, I suppose, but I was never invited into her house; nobody that I ever heard of was, but I wouldn't have thought a cask of gold worth the nervous misery that visit caused me. My worst encounter with her, however, belongs to another story.

When Mr Scott retired and Mr Moore came as colleague and successor, Mr Moore refused to occupy the manse till alterations were made. Since it was the parish church the expense had to be borne by the heritors even if they belonged to another church. Mrs Archibald owned a good deal of property in Cromarty and she was furious. There was a good deal of bad feeling about it in other quarters too and some nasty letters were written to the *People's Journal*. One day when the *Journal* letters were particularly unpleasant Mrs Archibald saw Mr Moore in the distance, darted into a shop for a copy of the paper and when he came along she handed it to him saying, 'Read that and see what the Cromarty people think of you'.

William MacLeod was our gardener, which is a grandiloquent way of saying that he was a jobbing gardener who made himself responsible for our garden and the two bank ones. He was a dear little man, as brown as a nut and always quiet and happy. He wasn't a particularly good gardener but worked away, taking whiles of sitting in the tool shed. Helen sat there with him often – Wesmull's hoss, William's house, she called it. The extent of his erudition might be gauged from the fact that for a whole summer there was a notice in one of our borders, 'Sid son/Kandy Tuff.' The avenue was so long and wide that it took William two days in spring and other two in autumn to reduce it to order. He disliked the job so much that every time anybody passed him he said, 'As good to me be in the Perth penitentiary'. He sent in an account now and again but it was very moderate.

He was not only our gardener; he was also one of our elders and a most devoted attender at every service, including the prayer meeting. I don't know what elders do nowadays or whether there are any prayer meetings but in our time it was the custom for them to take part in the meeting and even to address it if the minister was away from home. They arranged it amongst themselves, and as fishermen were ready speakers and loved taking meetings there was no difficulty about it. The only trouble was that they were apt to let their eloquence run away with them. My Uncle James was at a meeting once in the fishing village of Sandend and saw a fisherman pull the jacket of a friend who was engaged in prayer and heard him say, 'Sit doon! it's my shottie.'

I wouldn't like to give the impression that prayer meetings were comic occasions, but we had enough to do sometimes to keep serious. Poor William MacLeod wasn't funny so much as pathetic. He always started his prayers, 'We are gathered here in the place where prayer is wanted to be made.' He didn't aspire to preaching evidently for he only once took the prayer meeting and that was when your father was in France and I daresay even the fisher elders had more than their fill of taking meetings. William's address was chiefly about a man he had once known who was a thoroughly bad character. He committed all the ordinary sins and reduced himself and his family to poverty. Then he became converted and all was changed, and the address ended on a triumphant note, 'The last time I saw him he had an overcoat and an umbrella'.

James Reid's Cromarty accent led him astray, 'Lord, teach us to care for the (h)erring'.

But Robert Watson's eloquence was the most shattering. He sometimes prayed for 20 minutes, a word in a text would suggest another text and he went on and on. He carried his imagery to unheard of lengths. One night, praying about the vine and the branches, he became so enthused about the subject that he cried, 'Dig about us and dung us, Lord'. I heard him give an address on New Wine in Old Bottles. 'James Reid would tell you,' he said 'that if you patch a sail with new canvas the wind will tear the whole thing out. It's like that with new wine in old bottles. The woman of Samaria was dried up and done with sin and when Christ poured the new wine of the Gospel into her what happened? She burst and the Gospel flowed out of her to all her neighbours.' I can't imagine what his topic can have been when he said, 'Some men are verra bashful at the coortin, but the weemen will take them out for walks and get broches and brasslets!'

A Mr Ralph, a boatbuilder from Avoch, had a job in Cromarty during the war and came to our church and taught in the Sunday School. One evening at a Sunday School teachers' meeting he sat forward and said solemnly 'There's just one question I want to ask, Is this Sunday School effeminate with the Sunday School Union?'.

But to return to William MacLeod – we didn't think he had much comfort in his home. His wife was a big soft looking woman. I never even saw her till William fell ill. They had no family. When he got his flycup, which he took at his leisure in his 'hoss', and handed in his tray he always said, 'That tastit my hert'. Mrs MacLeod never left her house, not even to go to church with William. When he complained sorrowfully to Annie Leslie about people who didn't go to church, Annie, who didn't practise the finer courtesies, said, 'You needn't speak, your own wife doesn't go' and we felt that she had broken the bruised reed.

Mrs Grant who like ourselves went a good deal to see William when he was ill took him a rubber bottle – a novelty then. Next time he went back Mrs M had it close to the front of the fire heating it before she would put in the hot water.

William was no sooner dead than his widow became wonderfully lively, attended church twice a Sunday and prayer meeting on Thursday. So far as we knew she was left with nothing but the five shilling old age pension, and we gave her a good deal of help. When your father was in France I was often quite ill-off for help with the garden and if the weather was frosty it was impossible to open the potato pit. One day I met Mrs MacLeod in the town and she gave me a bitter complaint about having no potatoes. I told her we had none either, because we couldn't get the pit opened, but such as we had I would divide with her. Accordingly next morning I sent her a basketful: they were smallish but we were using them ourselves, having nothing else. An hour later I found the basketful on the back door steps. David Taylor came to the door and I pointed them out to him. He said, 'Take no notice. Mrs MacLeod's an awful queer woman.' I took no notice, to her or to anybody else but was much annoyed. The next time I went down town Mrs Archibald came out of her house and confronted me. She said she was sorry to hear that I had been so foolish as to send small potatoes to Mrs MacLeod. Small potatoes, she said, were only used by country people for seed, and an old country-woman would look upon a gift of them as an insult. I wish I could say that I quelled her with a look and made her apologise for her impertinence. Actually I have no recollection at all of what, if anything, I said to her.

One thing I do know, I never risked insulting Mrs MacLeod again. After I had confided the story to Mrs Malcolm and we had had a good laugh about it I felt better, but the incident did nothing to boost my ego. I owe to William MacLeod the finest compliment that was ever paid to me. When the commissioners from Glasgow Presbytery came to Chanonry Presbytery to prosecute the Eastpark call to your father, Thomas Middleton was the Cromarty elder who did the speech making. When he had finished paying eloquent tribute to your father, he said, 'As for Mrs MacLean I can't do better than tell you what was said by an old elder of ours, William MacLeod. Somebody, knowing that he worked in the garden and about the house, said to him, 'What like is your minister's wife?' 'I'll just tell you what she's like,' said William, 'She's no neen ahin himsel'.'

Before I went to Cromarty my predecessor, Mrs Gauld, had warned me that Mrs Mackay, secretary of the Women's Guild, had been a thorn in her flesh, and that if I didn't put my foot down etc etc. Mrs Mackay was certainly a redoubtable character but, not being the ideal minister's wife and never having had the urge towards leadership, I was willing to let her do as much of the work as she liked, so long as she did it well and was amenable to reasonable suggestions. She was an Aberdeenshire woman and I understand the breed if I don't always admire it. Moreover I was persona grata with Mrs Mackay before we met. She was a cousin of that Mrs Morgan who used to take all the youngsters of Thomson Street to picnic in Barclay's Woodie, and the Morgans had been so kind as to make their advance notices favourable. Incidentally, Alick Morgan, who first mentioned war to me, was at Nigg during the 1914–18 war with the Black Watch and used to come to see us. He was killed in France.

Mrs Mackay, when we knew her, was the widow of a doctor who had been Cromarty's sole medico for many years. She had been a teacher at Peddieston, four miles from Cromarty, and Dr Mackay a bachelor of 70 created a sensation by marrying her. A wealthy man, he boasted that his wedding cost him only half a crown. Her mother, Mrs Mackenzie, who had lived with her at Peddieston, moved into the doctor's house too. In our time she was very old and senile and it took courage to go and see her but she must always have been a terror. There were countless stories about her. When Dr Mackay died two of the teachers called and according to custom were taken to view the remains. Mrs Mackenzie did the honours and when they were standing beside the coffin she said with a backward wave of her hand, 'There he lies, a warrior taking his rest.' Then they went downstairs, and pointing to the portrait of burly, bearded Dr Mackay she said, 'This is the man that left us a' this grandeur.'

As she got older she became dangerous and would tell visitors what somebody said about them. Sometimes it was true but always hurtful. People complained not so much of Mrs Mackenzie but of Mrs Mackay who allowed her to say what she liked, never checked her, and never apologised for her. Mrs Scott called one afternoon and the old lady gave her a graphic account of a dreadful experience they had had with a lady, whom she named, and who had taken the most unheard-of liberties and had even stayed overnight and had wet the bed. Mrs Mackay sat quietly by and, when Mrs Scott left, went to the door with her. 'I'm so sorry' said Mrs S, 'that you had all that trouble'. 'Oh' was the reply 'that was all nonsense. We haven't had a visitor.' Only once did I hear her complain. She had a bad cold and I sympathised with her. 'I never have the chance to get rid of it,' she said, 'my mother will be out sometimes on the Braehead, screaming murder in the middle of the night and I have to go and fetch her in. She never takes cold but I do.'

There were a good many people of our acquaintance who belonged to a society that was even then disappearing and that didn't survive the war, the Grahams for instance. They were three elderly maiden ladies, the only survivors of a large and wealthy family who had a huge house at the east end of the town. They had lived in great style; Mr Bain, the draper and a Provost of Cromarty, had started life as a page boy with them. When we first knew them they had reduced their establishment to two or three servants but were living on the proceeds of antiques and jewellery and famous paintings. It was said that they had recently sold a Raeburn for £4,000.

They were charming ladies, full of kindness and good works but so helpless that I doubt whether any one of them ever washed a dish in her life. I was at tea with them one winter afternoon when the lamp began to smoke. They got excited and fluttered and were to ring the bell for the maid to come and do something about it when I bent forward and turned down the wick. 'How clever of you, dear Mrs MacLean!' they chorused, but I was uneasily conscious that I had lost caste by not waiting for the maid to climb two flights of stairs. It would have been more ladylike to be covered with specks of soot.

Miss Jane, the eldest, was considered a little peculiar in an aristocratic, ladylike way. The poorer people were firmly dealt with and their failings freely criticised. When Dannie Screech ran away from the poorhouse, she met him in the street and said, 'Dear me, Dannie, what are you doing here? I thought you were in the poorhouse.' A soldier standing by said, 'Who is that?' 'Ach,' said Dannie, 'she's just an old woman, as old as Hugh Miller.'

Mrs Scott, who had known the Grahams always, confided to me once that Jane was rather selfish. She never did anything she didn't like doing. When her parents were ill she refused to go near them, and when they died she refused to go and look at them in their coffins. That was an unforgiveable peculiarity in those days. The two younger Miss Grahams were incapable of arrogance or rudeness of any kind. Jane and Mrs Scott were quite frankly rude when they felt like it, very rude too, never to me.

Miss Nancy was different. She was sweet and gentle and everybody's favourite. I knew her well because we spent a week of afternoons together once a year. It was one of my duties to hand out money from a Trust Fund to 70 poor people – four shillings each they got. Miss Nancy's company was the only thing that made it bearable. She knew every single person in the fisher town whereas I could never distinguish between Mrs Watson Leezie, Mrs Watson Ovens and Mrs Watson Bodders. The Big Vennel and the Little Vennel were places of mystery to me. The Paye which was the oldest street in Cromarty was comparatively uninhabited then but it was proudly pointed out as having 'a croon o the causeway' – an arrangement of stones sloping up to the straight line of blocks which formed the centre line or crown of the road. It was also noteworthy as being the road down which fugitives from Culloden hurried on their way to the ferry which would take them across to Easter Ross and thence to their remote Highland fastnesses.

I loathed handing out money – it was equally hateful whether they took it shamefacedly, or eagerly closing a fist round it, or with fulsome compliments to the visitors – who weren't the givers! One wifie used to say that she looked forward to getting it so that she could buy a bottle of port and Miss Nancy was humorously doubtful whether she should get it for such a purpose.

Miss Henrietta, the youngest of the Grahams, was supposed to be the business-like one of the three though she was woefully incompetent by normal standards. She lived long after the other two and when I last saw her she had sold the family house and was living in a small house with no money except an allowance from a niece and a yearly grant from the Indigent Gentlewomen's Society. She didn't seem to have any objection to the house but it was said to be haunted and now stands empty. Last time we were in Cromarty it was being offered for £200 – a seven or eight roomed house – but there was no buyer. After Miss Graham left it people from Inverness bought it but they stayed in it a very short time because of strange noises and doors that opened and shut unaccountably. A lady then came to stay in it who vowed that after she had gone to bed and locked her door she could see the handle turning as if by someone turning it on the outside. She then got a huge watchdog and the first night it was in the house it howled so horribly that she cleared out the next morning, went straight to a solicitor in Inverness and asked him to sell the house for whatever it would fetch. After a long time a gentleman from the south came to see it and made all the preliminary arrangements for buying it but on the day he was to sign the papers he died in his car at the door of the solicitor's office.

Miss Henrietta latterly went to live at Forsyth House as a boarder and died there aged 93. The first Christmas we were in Aberdeen a box of large pan drops came by post with a note inside, 'For the children with best wishes from Henrietta Graham'. I had recognised the writing on the label but when I wrote to thank her she replied, 'I wish I had sent the sweets to the children but I sent no cards or presents this Christmas. I'm too old.'

9

STIR AND EXCITEMENT

Sunday in Cromarty was very much like any Sunday that you may remember in our house. Most of our time in Cromarty was so filled up with extra work that one day was much like another, except that Sunday had services. For example the staff of the Guild Hut – usually amounting to the superintendent, GF Barbour etc – and two students always had their Sunday dinner in our house. There would mostly be soldiers around at teatime and as the matron of the Military Hospital lived with us there was no Sabbath calm. The Guild Hut would have been in the First World War what a Naafi Hut was in the Second, but they were mostly run by churches, YMCA etc.

I used to think and still do that the feeling of getting from one high point to another was the bane of my life. Social meetings, Communions, Special Services, holidays – there seemed to be no respite. But many people, no doubt, lead a life of unthinkable monotony. In a sermon which I heard Principal Iverach preach in Cromarty, in July 1913, he said that when you are anxious, see if there's anything you can do about it, and having done it, leave it. His text was, 'Fear not, little flock, it is your Father's good pleasure to give you the Kingdom'. (James Iverach was Principal, 1905–22, of the Free Church College, Aberdeen, and UFC Moderator 1912–13)

During the War two ladies lived with us. Your sister Helen feared that she had been responsible for slight damage to a magazine belonging to them. She said she would like to go to bed. She said her prayers and added, 'Please let the ladies forget I tore their book.' She got into bed but sleep wouldn't come, so she got out and said her prayers again, but this time it was, 'Please let me forget I tore the ladies' book.' Helen preferred her father when things went wrong: 'Go away for my father,' she once said to me, 'he comforts me better when I've been bad.'

Visitors mean work and anxiety and expense and lost summer-time – all beyond calculation. Nobody knows that better than I do. But I had a servant, and if I hadn't money I was supported by the feeling that in a manse hospitality was top virtue. As for the expense, it has only begun with visitors – all the extras are lying around for months. There's no teacher like experience, but his fees are high.

My first servant was Annie Leslie who belonged to Rothiemay. Her sister, Mary, was a pupil of mine, a very nice girl, and I would have preferred her. Her aunt had told me that she meant to go into service, but when I sent a message via that aunt that I would be glad to take her with me I was told that there was an older sister, Annie, ready to leave home and that Mary was too young, so Annie it was. She was a strapping, good looking girl. The Leslies were all farmers, highly respected and moderately prosperous, and of a class which doesn't nowadays send its daughters to service. When Annie came to Nethybridge she was 17 and knew even less about domestic economy than I did, but we were both willing to learn. She was a member of the Haddo House *Onward and Upward Association* of which Lady Aberdeen was the founder and president (The Association was founded by Lady Aberdeen 'for the material, mental and moral elevation of women'). Mrs Forbes of Rothiemay was vice-president, and mistresses and servants in Banffshire and Aberdeenshire joined it in large numbers – 800 mistresses and 800 servants in its first year. The magazine connected with it came by post every month – *Onward and Upward* it was called – and it was practically a correspondence course in housekeeping. Annie read it from cover to cover, answered the questions and got prizes for papers on How to Set a Table and How to Make a Bed and such-like details of housework. In course of time she became an excellent servant and people who didn't have to live with her envied me. Actually Annie was most of the time very pleasant company and if one hinted that her temper was unreliable people usually replied that good servants were always ill-tempered and that good-tempered ones were lazy. Experience has taught me that this is a fiction for which ill-tempered people are responsible.

Annie was with us for six years. She went to Cromarty with us after two years in Nethybridge. She hadn't admitted to thinking much of Nethy so long as we were there but, when we had settled in Cromarty, Nethy became very Heaven. Her happiness was always retrospective. Cromarty was so different from anything she had hitherto known, however, that she was interested and excited and there were a good many girls of her own age and occupation with whom she could be friendly. One of them, Nellie Forbes, was with Provost and Mrs Ross at the Commercial Bank, and when your sister Helen was old enough to go down town Annie and she spent a great many afternoons at the Bank House.

There was a biggish family of the Leslies, seven or eight I think, and for some reason which I never understood Annie was very much ashamed of it. When the last one was born, after we were in Cromarty, she was so angry that she wept bitterly and refused to write her mother. However, she got a letter saying they hadn't made up their minds what to call the baby, so we discussed it together, decided on Johann and the breach was healed. She had a real Aberdeenshire habit of speech, brusque to the point of rudeness, and her terse comments could be pretty deflating. I remember her saying about a friend who had got a muff, 'I wouldn't care to go along the street with my hands before me'.

When the war came and Cromarty was full of sailors and soldiers, and all available houses were filled with officers' families, Annie's sister, Mary Leslie, came to be housemaid to a naval officer's family. Annie was a nice-looking girl but Mary had become so unusually pretty that we were constantly being asked by visitors, 'Who is that extraordinarily handsome girl who sits beside your servant in church?' She was a gentle, pleasant girl and for quite a long time Annie was happy and her temper much improved. Mary spent all her off time with Annie. One evening I was doing something in the kitchen when they were looking through a Christmas parcel that had come from home. Mary was reading out the letter that came with it. 'This scarf is the latest fashion', it said, and Mary laughed and said, 'What would she say if she saw Bain's window?' Bain, the local draper, had got the old-fashioned small window of his shop replaced by a larger plate-glass window.

The 3rd Seaforths were stationed in Cromarty and their camp was quite near the Manse which swarmed with soldiers all the war years. Other Service people were at one stage camped and billeted on the Sutors. The officers' wives – they were all English – were the talk of Cromarty because they thought nothing of suggesting getting a half morning roll delivered to them.

We had a room set aside for such of our camp friends as cared to write their letters or read in it. They came and went as they liked and always got cocoa if they were there at 9 o'clock. There were others who came into the family circle, and Annie entertained her own set in the kitchen. Mr Hingley, a Wesleyan chaplain to the Fleet, lived with us for a couple of years and then was sent to another naval base. Your father and he spent all their spare time in the Guild Hut at the Camp.

All the stir and excitement began to affect Annie's never very sweet temper. We would be aware even before we got up in the morning that a day of trouble was upon us. She would bang about, knocking against things and making as much noise as if she were shifting furniture at a flitting. These bouts would last for two or three days and it was hardly safe to make a remark to her till she had returned to normal. We suspected that she had become enamoured of a certain Sgt Mackay, a Lewisman, and that the affair was not progressing to her satisfaction. Your father and Mr Hingley knew him and knew his reputation in the camp and Mr Hingley, being young and an Englishman, ventured to suggest to her that the said sergeant wasn't good enough for her. She received his remarks in dead silence and never referred to them; whether they achieved anything good or bad we never knew.

I suppose I lacked both authority and experience but Annie's tantrums began to get me down. She managed to behave with civility in your father's presence and she never neglected her work, on the contrary the worse her temper the harder she worked but she was often extremely rude to me and went out of her way to annoy me. Early in 1916 we decided that in view of the fact that we expected a baby in May it would be a good idea to give Annie a holiday. Accordingly she went to Rothiemay for a fortnight. We heard afterwards that her mother said they couldn't understand how I was putting up with her and they were glad to see her go away again.

While she was away I had a slight accident. I was working with the kitchen range which was an enormous affair with two ovens when the bottom fell out of it and in struggling to lift the front and dispose of the redhot coal I hurt my back. I threatened a miscarriage and had to stay in bed for a week or two. I don't remember how we managed till Annie came back but there was no difficulty about getting work done. There were plenty of soldiers' wives only too glad to oblige and we already had had several of them about. One of them brought a little boy with her, and one day when he drank a whole bottle of face lotion she carried on as if we kept a poisoner's establishment in order to poison her child, and never came back.

Annie, unfortunately, was not improved by her holiday and we had decided to dispense with her services at the summer holidays but she forestalled us. One day in a fit of temper she told me she was leaving, went down town and engaged herself as cook to an officer's wife and came back and told me she would be starting her new job in a week's time. She was still in the house when Alasdair was born.

Alasdair was born on May 2, 1916 and the nurse had been engaged for the 16th. However, all the nurses in the military hospital were our good friends and several of them took over till our own nurse came. The doctor said I wasn't able to nurse the baby and he was bottle fed from the first. I always regretted it. We got our milk from the Scotts. They had a cow and had more milk than they could use, but it was a private arrangement and their milk wasn't tested. (Alasdair died on 12 November 1916. Mother believed that a lot of infection came to Cromarty with the First World War, not least because rats came ashore from Navy ships and could be seen making their way into the town)

We were surprised to hear a few months later that Annie was getting married to John Reid, the son of Sandy Reid who had recently died and had been one of our elders. John was a very nice young man. He was in the Merchant Navy and was so seldom at home that we couldn't understand how Annie knew him at all. Moreover, the Reids were all fisher folk and they were practically a separate community in Cromarty. It turned out that John Reid had been told when he came home to his father's funeral that old Sandy had said, 'I wish I saw Johnnie married to a nice girl like that one they have at the Manse.' They had only met twice, or so it was said, before they got married in Aberdeen. They had a flat or rooms in Rose Street. Annie went several times to see my mother whom of course she had often met in our house. John Reid died in the influenza epidemic at the end of the war when their baby girl was only five weeks old, and Annie was left penniless. She got no pension because his death had nothing to do with the war.

Annie went home to Rothiemay but got on so badly with her parents that she wrote Nellie Forbes asking her to find out whether we would be willing to take her back. Mrs Ross came up to see me and plead her cause and several other people seemed to think it would be a good idea to take her back. Your father would have been willing, but for once in my life I was adamant. There had been no direct communication between us but I understood that she wanted to bring the child and knowing Annie I could see no prospect of being able to cope with such a situation, especially since I couldn't rid myself of the feeling that she had a good deal of responsibility for Alasdair's having been delicate.

Willie Leslie, her oldest brother, then went into a farm of his own in Rothiemay and took Annie with him, and that arrangement lasted for a year or two when he announced that he was getting married and she had to look for another job. She went as housekeeper to a widower in Insch, but the brother didn't marry after all. In course of time Annie married the widower who was 39 years older than herself. He died some years ago at the age of 95. Several years ago I met Mr and Mrs Douglas Matheson in Cromarty. Douglas is now Science master in Invergordon but before their marriage they both taught in Insch and lodged with Mrs Trap – Annie. They said she spoke a lot about me but whether well or ill I don't know.

At the end of the war Mary Leslie married an orderly in the Military Hospital. He was a miner in Fife and apart from the fact that she had a large family I never heard anything more of her. I know two elderly bachelors in Cromarty who still speak nostalgically of bonnie Mary Leslie.

To return to Cromarty manse – when Annie announced that she meant to leave me in the lurch I wrote to Mrs Shepherd, my Rothiemay landlady, to ask if she knew anybody who would come to our assistance. The local Cromarty girls were all very gainfully employed, and in any case we didn't want a local girl. Mrs Shepherd didn't know of anybody but lent me her daughter Maggie, a former pupil of mine, till I had time to make other arrangements. Maggie stayed with us till we went on holiday in July and was all that I could have wished for, but she barely counts as a servant. We had a visit yesterday (1963) from Maggie Shepherd and her sister Winnie, Mrs Turner, the daughters of my Rothiemay landlady. Maggie comes now and again to see me but I hadn't seen Winnie since she was six years old, 53 years ago. She says she remembers me well, the blouses I used to wear and how she used to cross the bridge to meet me when I was coming out of school. It's nice to be kindly remembered after all these years.

It was only after the First World War that ordinary people became holiday-minded. A few days with and on relatives were the normal procedure. On that July holiday in Aberdeen I set about looking for somebody to take back to Cromarty but servants were already in 1916 almost impossible to find. Mrs Ross, an acquaintance of my mother's, and a woman so peculiar that she deserves a book to herself, gave me the address of a girl who would, she said, be the perfect servant. I wrote the damsel suggesting that we might meet and discuss the matter, and she replied in a lengthy rambling letter which said neither yes nor no. She did however sign it, 'Your sister in God,' so I replied saying that I had made other arrangements.

We had promised Mrs Shepherd to go from Aberdeen to Contin via Rothiemay and stay for a day or two, and I found my next servant there. She was Maggie Cormack, another of my pupils, at home recuperating after an illness, Mrs Shepherd had already made sure that she was willing to go with us. She had been between-maid at Fasque, the Gladstones' Kincardineshire house.

Maggie had been unremarkable as a pupil but she was by far the best servant I ever had. I learnt a good deal from her. Your father used to say she was so smart it was a pleasure to see her moving about, and she did everything as if it made her happy to do it. She stayed with us nearly two years and left because she was ill. She was several times ill when she was with us, but the Cromarty doctor vowed there was nothing wrong with her. He must have been mistaken because she never had good health and died before she was 30. After we went to Glasgow Maggie came several times to see us. She had married a man she met in Cromarty; he was a soldier then and they were the merest acquaintances, but they met again in Glasgow after the war and recognised each other. He was a compositor in the Glasgow Herald. Then they left Glasgow and I lost touch with her, but her mother called on me once when she was on holiday in Glasgow, and I heard later from Mrs Shepherd that Maggie had died.

When your father left for France on 15 January 1918, Roddie was a month old and Maggie Cormack was still with us, but left in the spring, early in March if I remember rightly. Many a dreary night I spent in Cromarty manse when your father was in France and Roddie howling the house down. I'm glad to think I never drugged my babies or myself.

The whole set-up at the time was difficult; servants, as we had hitherto understood that name, couldn't be got; the manse was to be occupied by two sets of ministers' families in July and August and I was to be in Aberdeen. I made do therefore with a young girl who lived at a nearby farm. Her name was also Maggie. Her mother had recently died after a long illness during which time Maggie had left school and worked at home. She had scarcely taken up residence when I realised how wise we had been to avoid having local girls as servants. Maggie's father was a farm grieve. There were three families of Middletons and amongst them they owned all the farms of any consequence in the district. They were very fine people, ardent supporters of the UF Church and they admired your father exceedingly. In his absence I could hardly tell them that the girl they had recommended so highly was what we would now call a juvenile delinquent. For one thing she ate enormously. Nothing was safe from her – cooked or raw. For the only time in my life I was compelled to keep things under lock and key, and then she displayed the utmost ingenuity in searching out the keys. She also stole everything that was movable – toys, books, food and clothes. When asked if she had seen such and such she answered with a prolonged 'No-o-oh'. At first sight she was astonishingly handsome until it became evident that she was half-witted.

Maggie Brown, Mrs Macdonnell, came from Inverness to spend her Easter holidays with me and had the most diverting time. Every morning Maggie the servant went for the milk and was away for about half an hour. We then went to her bedroom and collected all the things she had stolen since the previous morning. If she noticed that they were away she took no trouble about it — a fresh lot replaced them. One morning Maggie B pointed out that there were prune stones lying on the unmade bed. I declared that she couldn't have got them in our house. Roderick Matheson had said to me a few days before that he had prunes and could let me have a pound. There were no points in the First War, and very little rationing. I had brought home my precious prunes, put them in the linen cupboard at the top of the stairs and put the key in one of the small drawers of my dressing table. We went forthwith for the key and sure enough only three or four prunes remained. Without the flicker of an eyelid Maggie vowed that she had never seen key or prunes and didn't know who had put the stones in her bed.

She wore my new stockings and put them back in the drawer when they were worn out. I was reduced to carrying all possible keys on my person. Alick Mackenzie, Nethybridge, who was by that time a minister came for the month of April to take charge of the congregation. He found Maggie's appetite a perpetual entertainment. One day I made a beefsteak pie and Alick said, 'There's enough of that for tomorrow's dinner.' 'Not if it's put where Maggie can get at it,' I said. I agreed reluctantly to put it in the pantry and prove my statement. Alick went back and fore to the pantry all afternoon and reported progress. By teatime there was no need for his visits, the pie was finished. After that he used to say that he understood now what had always puzzled him, that their cock at home never seemed to want food till he saw the hens eating it. On the same principle he ate twice as much as usual so that there would be none left for Maggie.

I was on the point of despair when the Grahams, the three old maiden ladies, let their house to General Hunter Blair and asked me if I would give house-room to their old cook, Mrs Fraser. She had no home but with them and they wanted to reserve her services till their return. I found that the ministers who were coming for July and August were glad to have her services too, so that was settled. I didn't put Maggie away but explained the situation to Mrs Fraser who was an old woman with plenty of experience. She took entire charge of the food and I had more time to be watchful elsewhere.

When I went with Helen and Roddie to Aberdeen for July and August I dispensed gladly with Maggie's services and told her that she had better get something to do because two months would be too long for her to be idle. After I went back to Cromarty Dolly and Annie Middleton called one day and said they were thinking of taking Maggie into their home as under-housemaid. They asked what I had thought of her and I said I had not found her at all satisfactory, but didn't venture to say that she wasn't honest. They said that Harriet, their head housemaid, was very competent and eminently fitted for training young servants so they felt quite happy about the situation. We left Cromarty in January of 1920 and it was more than 30 years before I heard of Maggie again.

I went to Inverness one day in 1953 to meet Miss Fleming. When we met her she told us that as she stepped off the bus a woman with three children came up to her and said, 'Hello, Miss Fleming, do you remember me, Maggie? I used to see you often when I was at the manse in Cromarty.' Miss Fleming thought her face familiar but had no time to ask questions because the woman was hurrying for the train to London where she said she lived. The description didn't sound like Maggie who was the only servant I had had whom I couldn't, so to speak, put my finger on. The incident, however, set me to enquiring about her. The family had evidently been away from the district for a long time. It seemed that the whole family had Maggie's failing. The first to be discovered was a sister who had been stealing persistently over a long period in a local office. Captain Morrison of Navity was going home late one night when he noticed very strange goings-on at the farm where Maggie's father was grieve. The farm-house was unoccupied. A large load of farm stuff was being driven away by people from Cromarty fisher-town whose reputation was very unsatisfactory. He mentioned the matter to Frank Middleton: a watch was kept on the farm from a smiddy nearby and it was established beyond all doubt that Maggie's father had carried on systematic stealing for years. He was dismissed and the whole family left the district.

Maggie's career had been what might unfortunately have been expected. She had gone to Perth as a housemaid. She wasn't there long. She went all gay in Perth, attended dances galore dressed in the evening gowns and silk stockings of her employers, and didn't even bother to cover her tracks. The gowns etc would be dumped over chairs in her bedroom when they went to look for them. When the Second World War started she joined the Women's Services, made an unsatisfactory marriage, and had a child which died in infancy. The husband disappeared and at the time of my enquiries Maggie was working in an Inverness restaurant as dish-washer and general cleaner. I thought of making an errand into the restaurant but never did it.

When I went back to Cromarty at the end of August 1918 Mina W from the fisher-town came by the day. Not only did she want to be home at night but I couldn't face the prospect of having her on my hands all the time. I expected very little of her but was thankful to get anybody who was vouched for. She had been working for the Bains for several years and Mrs Bain said she was honest and reliable but very slow. Actually I had never heard of slow-motion but I saw plenty of it with Mina. She arrived at some unearthly hour in the morning. I was supposed to rise in time to open the door for her but rather than go through the huge house in the dark or, what was almost worse, with a candle, I left it unlocked at night. It was a heavy front door and we were well off the beaten track.

Mina worked all day and was never finished. She could scrub and sweep and dust and wash quite efficiently in course of time, but nobody who hadn't seen Mina in action – so-called – could believe how long a time it is possible to take to fill a kettle and put it on a fire. Fortunately I wasn't so busy as formerly. The Seaforth camp was gradually emptying, and fewer gunboats were coming into the Firth, which meant that not only were there fewer soldiers and sailors to entertain, but there was an end to the constant stream of official visitors, most of whom had taken it for granted that hospitality, and if need be lodgings, awaited them in the Manse.

Mina had the genuine Cromarty accent which is quite unlike the speech of the fisher folk round the Moray Firth. The Cromarty people speak in a kind of gentle sing-song and confuse their aspirates. 'Be a good boy Roddie,' Mina would say, 'and we'll 'ave a walk hup the havenue'. She was pleasant, willing, obliging, entirely free of aggressiveness, but practically mindless. To carry on a conversation with her was impossible. There was a municipal election in Cromarty which for some forgotten reason was causing a good deal of excitement. On the evening of voting day, when Mina came in to set the supper I said to her 'I wonder who'll be top of the poll.' 'I don't know,' she said, 'Likely it'll be him 'at 'as the most votes.' We worked peaceably together till the time came for us to leave Cromarty and parted without rancour on either side. A good many years later Mina married a man from the Black Isle. Presumably they lived an unhurried life together. On our recent visits to the old district we often saw her. She is a widow now, childless, and apparently as unexcited and unexciting as ever.

To Glasgow we took Katie from Rosemarkie. We were known to be looking out for a servant and she was recommended to us as being all that one asks for.

Soon after we had settled in Cromarty we were told by sailors and officers of the fleet with whom we became friendly that there was going to be war between us and the Germans. We just didn't believe it. The Enchantress lay overnight in the Firth just below our windows and Cromarty was agog with speculation. Winston Churchill was on board and was having a meeting with the Admirals but we were only pleasantly interested.

We were on holiday in Aberdeen in 1914 when the Territorials were called up, and we left for Cromarty on the morning of August 4th. What a queer journey that was! It took the whole day; Aberdeen about 9 am, dinner at Inverness, tea at Invergordon, and then across the 6 mile ferry to Cromarty. Since the Fleet was in Cromarty there was a general expectation that the German navy would make straight for it. We wondered whether our house would be still standing. Helen was two years old, dressed from head to heel in white – there were no pantaloons or sensible coloured clothes for children – and by the time she had spent most of the day on the floors of railway carriages she looked as if she hadn't been washed for months.

Cromarty was in a state of intense activity. We had first-aid classes, got our spare rooms ready to receive casualties, drew up lists of the blankets and bedding we could spare and were altogether as excited and unhappy as possible. By the time casualties did come, hospital huts had been got ready. A German submarine was sighted in the Firth one day and a dreadnought opened fire on it. The noise of firing was pretty alarming. Little Willie Stevenson at Peddieston was out on the moor with his sister when it began. He lay down on his face and she said to him, 'Are you frightened?' 'No,' he said 'but I've a terribly sore stomach.'

(Fear of a different kind gripped some of the newcomers to Cromarty during the war. When George Ross of Pitkerie had bought the estate of Cromarty in the late eighteenth century he brought work and people to Cromarty by establishing cloth, nail and spade factories, a lace industry and a brewery. Many of the workers were Gaelic-speaking Highlanders, some of them dislodged from their home country by the disintegration of the clan system and by the early clearances. For them Ross provided a Gaelic Chapel, the remains of which stand on the Kirky Brae above Cromarty. The chapel had fallen into disuse by the beginning of the twentieth century but it still had its roof. So after war broke out the Army took over the chapel as a billet for some Derby men, mostly youngsters from Glasgow. Those youths who had known only city life did not appreciate the building as their Highland predecessors had done. My mother told of how in the evenings they went down into the town to sink their sorrows in liquor. Then they staggered out, their imaginations invigorated but their spirits chilled, to face the terror of the dark journey up the hill, through the graveyard and into the decaying Gaelic chapel. A mutiny of sorts was threatened until they were accommodated in tents. Still they did not look on Cromarty as home from home, and it was with a sense of escape that they received word of their move to France).

HMS *Natal* was blown up one day near Christmas 1915 when there was a large party of civilians on board for a cinematograph entertainment. All the civilians were killed and hundreds of the sailors. There were funerals in Cromarty nearly every day for a long time, as the bodies were found by divers. One whole family, Marcus Dods, son of the Marcus Dods whose name must be very familiar to you (latterly, 1907–9, Principal of New College, Edinburgh), factor of an estate in Invergordon and his wife and family were all aboard. *The Press and Journal* (September 1961) has published an account of a book by Cecil Hampstead, *They Called it an Accident*, which has an account of the sinking of the *Natal* at Cromarty. 'After a series of loud explosions it sank, a blazing ruin, into the Firth'. I must be one of the very few people now alive who actually saw the Natal sink, and so far from being a blazing ruin there wasn't even a puff of smoke.

Moreover, nobody on the Cromarty side of the Firth heard a sound at all. On the Invergordon side there had been a certain amount of noise. (Mother often told of her witnessing the sinking of the *Natal*. A sailor from the *Natal*, George Laird, who had been a neighbour of Mother's in Aberdeen, came that afternoon on shore leave to visit Mother at the UF manse: the two of them were standing outside the manse talking to one another. Suddenly the sailor exclaimed, 'The *Natal*'s away.' Mother thought he meant that it had sailed out of the Firth. She looked over the hedge towards where it had been and saw two neat halves of it folding in towards one another and settling into the water – to rest, salvage reports were later to tell – on her funnels and gun turrets. Mother and George Laird hadn't heard a sound. Lines of graves up beside the Gaelic Chapel, and near to our family grave, mark the resting places of a number of those whose bodies were washed ashore)

I remember the day I was going down the Manse Brae into Cromarty when I met somebody who told me that Kitchener had been drowned and I felt that the bottom had fallen out of the world. Then your father went to France for a year's chaplaincy. He left at 5.30am on a dark January morning and was in the front-line trenches within a week. My mother and I were standing at the gate looking over the Firth at 11am on 11 November 1918 when all the ships in it blew their sirens because Armistice was signed. Mr Scott had come across the night before to tell us that he had got the news from the Camp. There was no wireless then. I can still feel the strange mixture of hope and loneliness and sadness with which I listened to the sirens.

Your father came home in January 1919, and we went to Glasgow in January 1920. The year between was very unsettled. The Seaforth Camp was disbanded, the Fleet left the Firth, there was no fishing because the boats had been commandeered and not yet returned. The North Sea was full of mines, and the boats that used to bring the coal supply couldn't get through. We were often seriously short of coal.

The last time I was in Cromarty, Lily Bain took me upstairs in their four-storey house to see attic bedrooms that had been decorated and had storm windows put in to replace skylights. The windows looked out over the fishertown and she remarked that it had not formerly been advisable to have an outlook in that direction because the fishertown had been so smelly and dirty. The fisherwomen had all sat mending their nets at their front doors. Nowadays their houses are all gaily painted, they have flower boxes in their windows and gardens at their front doors and the fisher town is a place of beauty. But no fishing boat leaves Cromarty. Before 1914 the fishing boats went out every evening and returned in the morning in time to send the fish to the London market. The First War damaged Cromarty's trade, the second one finished it. When we were in Cromarty we could get a good-sized codling for eightpence, so fresh that it was still jumping around. Now the Cromarty people buy their fish from a van that comes from Avoch. They have flowers instead of fish.

10

Buckingham Terrace to Haddock Avenue

We had been told that a large flat was waiting for us in Queen Margaret Drive. Eastpark U F Church had never had a manse. The housing shortage had begun and 'our' flat was occupied by a schoolmaster who had been appointed to a school in Edinburgh. He couldn't get a house in Edinburgh, therefore he couldn't vacate the Glasgow one and was still in it a year after we went to Glasgow by which time we had got a house for ourselves.

In the meantime your father was inducted at Eastpark in January 1920, and I took Helen, Roddie and Barbara, three weeks old, to Aberdeen. We were there for five or six weeks and then went to Glasgow and lodged with Miss Bain and her aunt Mrs Dewar. Katie from Rosemarkie joined us there, stayed with friends and came daily to help, chiefly to take Roddie and Barbara out, and to get messages. We were very happy with Miss Bain and Mrs Dewar but the quarters were rather cramped; we had only two rooms. One of them had a bed recess in it, a modern version of the old box-bed. It was study, dining room and living room as well as bedroom, and there were five of us! When Roddie, two years old, got in amongst your father's papers and tore up a whole set of Bible-class lectures we decided that we couldn't wait for the schoolmaster to move and must get on the move ourselves.

I noticed that a house in Buckingham Terrace was for sale and induced your father to go and ask the solicitors if they would let it to us for a year. It had been empty for seven years! Only my ignorance of Glasgow dirt gave me the courage. The solicitors consented and so did the Eastpark Deacons' Court. We got the house – five storeys – scrubbed from garret to basement, sent to Cromarty for our furniture and settled in. By the time we had cleaned and occupied the house for a year it sold without difficulty but we didn't get commission on the sale.

When we went to Glasgow in 1920 the Depression was at its worst, and a great many of the Eastpark people were idle. But I don't remember being particularly affected by it, perhaps because the people were strangers to us and the whole way of life was new, so that we expected nothing else.

Katie was quite a good servant but of a different class, if one may use that word, from Annie Leslie and Maggie Cormack. She was very unlike Mina Watson, not only were her movements normally speedy but her feelings were many and loudly expressed. If she went to the pictures she was always amazed and entranced and I had to listen to a detailed description of every picture she saw.

The Buckingham Terrace house was a monument of unworkableness. It had five storeys, three of them had two very large and one small room each, the top one had four attics and the basement two nice rooms – the kitchen and one we fed in when we hadn't company – besides black holes which in bygone years had housed servants. There was also a coal cellar with no light in it. One day Katie went into this cellar without bothering to take a candle, pushed in her shovel and brought out a load of coal with a double set of dentures reposing on the top. There was a gap in the top set which gave it a most macabre look. Wild shrieks brought everybody in the house rushing downstairs to find Katie in hysterics. Nothing, she declared, would induce her to enter that cellar again in case she might find the rest of the body. The previous occupant had been a dentist and the attics had been left in strange disorder. Quantities of loose teeth and dental plates at all stages littered the floors. One room was fitted up with mechanical appliances which I never examined but Helen and Roddie had a glorious time amongst them.

Katie wasn't without a sense of humour. She could laugh hilariously and tell quite funny stories but she was touchy and wasn't always amused. She was telling us something one day about the Society of Oddfellows in Rosemarkie and your father said he supposed there were quite a few odd fellows in Rosemarkie. She was most annoyed and never forgave him for it. If any remark was made which gave her the chance she always said, 'Even if Mr MacLean doesn't think much of Rosemarkie people'.

Buckingham Terrace to Haddock Avenue

Roddie was at the stage when he still occupied the high chair at mealtimes. No sooner would he be firmly fixed into it than he announced that he wanted to go to the bathroom, so it became the custom to enquire how matters stood before he was hoisted. One day Katie was finishing the setting of the dinner when your father said, 'Have you been to the bathroom Roddie?'. 'No' he said, 'but Katie has!' She felt that she was disgraced for life. She went next day to visit a friend in Rutherglen – a Mrs Bauchope – and to her she told the story. A number of visitors, including two young men, came in and Mrs B couldn't resist the chance. She told them the story, but by that time Katie had decided that it was funny.

She had a really annoying habit. Every time I was especially busy with visitors she had an acute attack of bile. There was no doubt about the genuineness of the attack, but why it happened so conveniently for her and inconveniently for me was a mystery. Professor James Stalker was with us once for nearly a week and in all that time Katie was confined to her room having severe sick turns. It was shortly after this that the Eastpark folk bought a house in Lansdowne Crescent. Our year in Buckingham Terrace had expired and we moved into the Manse.

At the flitting we discovered that a bottle of whisky that we supposed to have been unopened was not only opened but empty. Some time before we left Cromarty Willie M, who had followed us from Nethy and was working with the butcher, had arrived at our door one Saturday night terribly drunk. Your father did his best to get him sobered and he was kept in the house over the week-end. A bottle of whisky that was in his pocket was confiscated and never returned to him. When we were in Mrs Dewar's, Roddie took Miss Bain to look at it where I had put it in the bottom of the wardrobe drawer.

When we went on holiday to Boat of Garten, Katie went to Rosemarkie and from there she wrote to say she wanted to get a place nearer home and we thankfully accepted her decision though it was some time later that Helen cleared up both mysteries, not knowing of their existence. Katie, it seemed, had given her advice. If she wanted to be too ill to go to school – at exam times, say – she should eat raw suet and then she would be sure to have bile. 'That's what I do when your

129

mother's going to have visitors'. Then when better health was in order a good glass of whisky would do the trick.

It must have been from a registry office that I got Annie D. She was 16 or so and had never been out working before. Her mother had died when she was quite young and her father had kept the house and the family together. An older sister kept house till Annie left school, then Annie took her turn of house-keeping. She was extraordinarily good-looking in a gipsyish fashion, smart and well dressed, though she came from the Glasgow slums. We didn't want to have a girl staying in the house. I had no lack of baby sitters – lion tamers was our name for them, Mrs Stein and Miss Campbell, your two aunts Helen and Bella, Mary Urquhart, and others were available.

Annie was a strange, secretive girl. She was a good worker, obliging and civil but completely detached. I never found out much about her and she took no apparent interest in our affairs. Soon after she came to us a new milk-boy came. The dairy was quite near us. I remarked to her several times that he seemed a nice boy and different from the usual run of messengers. He had been coming for months before I discovered by the merest accident that he was her brother. 'Why did you never tell me, Annie' I said, 'that the milk boy is your brother?' 'I didn't think you would be interested' she said. The children neither liked nor disliked her so far as we were aware. She took little notice of them so they weren't tempted to spend time in her company. When she had been with us nearly two years she asked if we would be willing to have her stay in the house altogether. Her father, she said, didn't want to keep a home together any longer because they were all working and able to look after themselves. If Annie got a place where she could stay he would go into lodgings.

We weren't anxious to have her but we were on the point of going to Boat-of-Garten for a month and didn't like the idea of leaving her to knock about Glasgow Green whilst we were enjoying ourselves in the Highlands. She had never been in the country and wanted to come, so we postponed the major decision. At closer quarters she was no more friendly than before, and had a disconcerting habit of claiming her afternoon off and disappearing for hours. One day she said she was going to Carrbridge to visit a relation of one of their neighbours in

Glasgow. If she knew anything about this person she didn't own up to it. When midnight came and she hadn't returned we got worried. By 3.00am we had decided to get in touch with the police which we would probably have done earlier if it hadn't meant cycling three miles to Boat of Garten. She walked in quite unconcerned, had been kept late and didn't think it would take so long.

At Croftnagaren where we were staying there was a Glasgow boy – one of the boarded out children – who herded the cows and did odd jobs. This boy asked Mrs Cameron one day to tell me that Annie ill-used the baby – Isabel. He had seen her take the baby out of the pram and smack it. I had difficulty in believing this and asked Annie about it. She vowed that the boy was telling lies to spite her for something, and we dismissed the matter from our minds but saw to it that she wasn't left alone with the pram. At the same time we decided that she was too much of a responsibility and said she had better look out for a place where she could stay all night.

We parted on good terms but heard nothing of her for more than two years. You were an infant not quite a year old when she called one night and asked if we would take her back. It happened that I was looking for more help than a charwoman could give, Annie was prepared to promise anything and we agreed to take her. Everything went well so far as we knew for several months. There were a few unhappy incidents, chiefly concerned with her late hours. One night she didn't come in at all, but her explanation, if true, seemed reasonable enough. Then one evening your father and I were to go to the golden wedding celebrations of an Eastpark couple, Mr and Mrs Murchison. We were dressed and ready to go, and I had got you ready for the night and called for Annie to come and take charge of you. As soon as I put you into her arms you screamed and straightened out as stiff as a rod. I rushed to the sink and held your head under the cold water tap, and you came round and were violently sick. Your father wasn't present and you had come round by the time he got downstairs but my going to the party was out of the question though we never dreamt of associating Annie with the fit. The doctor said 'teething' and that was that. The same thing happened several times but nobody but myself happened to be present, and your father and Dr Gray quite frankly thought and said I was unduly alarmed, that it didn't amount to being a fit, you were perfectly healthy etc etc.

We went to Yetholm that year for July and August. Your father wasn't on holiday in July but came with us for a week and then came back for the second month. Annie was with us, but by this time I suspected her, was careful not to leave you alone. She was, however, troublesome in other ways. The first night we were there, though she had never been within 80 miles of the place before, she went out for a walk and came back on the pillion of a man's motor cycle after 11.00 pm. I told her I couldn't be responsible for her if she was to behave like that and would send her back to Glasgow if it happened again, and that she must be in the house by 10 o'clock. Thereafter, if she went out and happened to return at 9.30 she sat on the garden wall till the clock struck ten.

An old lady, a Mrs Scott, lived in the house next door and was interested in all the family. I told her about your queer turns and she said her oldest son had been the same and they discovered that the servant they had had had beaten him. However, there had been no incident since we left Glasgow, and the first Sunday in August we all set out for church intending to leave you with Annie. Your father was standing by when I put you in the pram and said, 'Look after him now Annie, we're going.' You just took one look at her and repeated the stiffening performance. That, you may be sure, was the last time. In all, I counted you had 13 of these turns – never one before Annie came, and never one after she left. The consideration now was on what pretext were we to get rid of her? A few nights later your father wakened up and said, 'There's a man in the house – I hear him speaking downstairs.' Annie slept in the room below us. I listened but could hear nothing but a loud beating in my own ears. He got up and went downstairs. As he reached the door he heard Annie speak, and the man and she both laughed aloud. He knocked, got no answer, then tried the door and found that it was locked. Next morning before breakfast he went downstairs and tackled Annie. She looked him in the eye and declared that there had been no man in the house, she had not heard him knock on her door and the door had not been locked.

He told her, but for the fact that she was homeless he would have sent her back to Glasgow that day, but she must set about looking for another place as soon as we got back. The affair was never mentioned between her and me, and she was never asked to explain your attacks. My mother said she had been much surprised to hear that we were taking her back after what happened about Isabel, but it is a fact, strange though it may seem, that we hadn't remembered that till she mentioned it. I have often wondered what became of Annie and whether she was reachable.

I have to go back now to the autumn of 1924 when Annie left us for the first time. We made up our minds to make do with a charwoman and got a Mrs A who lived in a close off Argyll Street. She was a widow and went out to work to augment her allowance from the Parish Council. There were some conditions attached to the time she could spend or the money she could earn because of her parish allowance but I forget what they were. At any rate I reckoned that she was worth a trial. She was what one might call 'a nice wifie' – not intelligent or competent or handsome but enough of all three to do my turn. Actually she served me very well for several years, off and on.

The first time she left she did so because she wanted me to take her daughter Nellie who was now due to leave school, and had to find something to do. If Nellie came to me, Mrs A would stay at home and look after her family and incur no suspicion from the parish authorities. Moreover if I took Nellie and trained her to work she could then apply for a place with a reference from me and without divulging her own address which was not genteel enough to recommend her if she had no other reference. It all seemed fair enough and I took Nellie and never regretted it, not because she was a good servant but because she was a unique character. Her work didn't count, one way or the other. She was strong and young and active and unfailingly good tempered, and her entertainment value was considerable. From the first she was eagerly sought after by the family. She was a fount of information of a kind that never came their way before.

Her address, she said, was Fish Penn, Argyle Street, but if she met any stranger and had to reveal it, she said Haddock Avenue because it sounded more genteel. The Penn was described as a square which was entered from an archway in Argyle Street and had houses all round it. Fascinating people, according to Nellie,

lived in these houses and the stories of their doings and mis-
doings filled our days with interest. The family had a lodger – a
tiddler. The word was new to us but Nellie explained that a
tiddler was a person, in this case a woman, who kept people's
money for them. The done thing, it seemed, was to save up for
Christmas and then start again to save for holidays. If you gave
the tiddler a shilling per week from July to December you
collected 25 shillings at Christmas, the other shilling – more
likely one and threepence – being the charge for having your
money kept out of your reach. Nothing would convince Nellie
that the Savings Bank would *give* money rather than take it
away. The kind of people who lived in Fish Penn didn't trust
Savings Banks. Having been introduced to tiddlers we began to
see paragraphs in the papers indicating that they weren't always
to be trusted either.

Sometimes Nellie's stories were serials with exciting instalments from day to day. One of the neighbours, a girl like herself,
was going to America. The Penn became the scene of farewell
festivities. Parties of incredible gaiety and variety took place at
frequent intervals. Then a day came when Helen, having been
sent to the kitchen for something, found Nellie in floods of tears.
'What's the matter Nellie?' she said but Nellie couldn't answer
immediately, not till the clock gave permission. This was the day
the friend was sailing for America and because Nellie was unable
to go to the pier to see her off she had promised that she would
cry from 5.0 to 5.30, the half hour that she would have spent in
lamentation along with the crowd. 'Surely you must be very fond
of her,' said Helen. 'Oh well,' was the reply, 'it wasn't that so
much, it was just that she was born and bred in the Penn.'

We began to suspect that Nellie's imagination was over-vivid
when she took to coming sometimes in the morning with a scarf
round her neck to hide the bruises. Her mother, she said, had a
fearful temper and resorted to violence if crossed. She gave
blood-curdling exhibitions of how she would be seized by the
neck and her mother would shout, 'I don't care if I swing for
you.' Marks on her neck bore witness to the truth of her stories.
They were never, of course, shown to me but knowing Mrs
Adams and considering that Nellie was about twice her size I
suggested that she was telling lies. Eventually she admitted that
she had made the bruises with black lead.

Buckingham Terrace to Haddock Avenue

After she had been with us about a year she declared that she was going to America. An uncle and aunt in Washington were going to adopt her. She was involved in so much business over her emigration that she was frequently an hour or so late in the morning. She seemed wonderfully knowledgeable and was full of talk about consuls and emigration officials, and even said that a mole on her neck was to be removed and she was much engaged in arrangements for the operation. Before that happened, however, an aunt, her mother's sister, grew ill and was taken to the Infirmary. Nellie found herself so much in demand for one thing and another connected with her aunt's illness that she was rarely in time for her work and couldn't concentrate on it when she was. Then one afternoon she arrived, her face swollen with weeping, and said she hadn't been able to come in the forenoon because her aunt had died and she had had to scrub out her house to have it ready for the remains coming home. Asked if her aunt had no family she said, Yes, a son and daughter, but they were useless at any time and were now overcome with grief.

I couldn't bring myself to say that I didn't believe a word of her story, but said that from now on she must come in time or stay away altogether. She didn't come back and I thought we had seen and heard the last of Nellie. In about a fortnight's time Mrs A arrived at the door, full of apologies for having come but she felt she had to find out what had happened. Nellie had gone home and said that I had gone to Leitholm for a long holiday and said I wouldn't need her till I came back. I hadn't given her any wages and had made no arrangement to give her any. Mrs A thought it was very unlike me to behave so oddly and after a fortnight of having Nellie at home idle she decided to come and ask me about it. A very much edited account of Nellie's ongoings shocked her, and when I said, 'Tell me this. Did your sister die a few weeks ago?' she collapsed. 'Oh,' she wailed, 'what would my sister say if she heard that? She was in the washhouse with me this morning.'

We arranged that Mrs A would come back to us and Nellie would keep house at home. That worked quite well for a while, but the Parish Council made trouble again and Nellie had to look for a job and her mother to look after her own house. The last we heard of Nellie she was working in a dish factory. All the faulty dishes were thrown out and it was Nellie's job to smash them. Your father said he never heard of anyone being more suitably employed.

From this time till Annie came back again we had Florrie Urquhart and Mrs B. The Urquharts were Cromarty people, Mr U being a keeper on the Rosehaugh estate. When he died Mrs Urquhart came to live in Glasgow. Mary Urquhart was already there and had been a member of Eastpark and an intimate friend of the family for several years. Florrie hoped to go in for nursing but wasn't old enough and was looking for a preliminary kind of job looking after children. She was a godsend to us, kept the household together when I was in hospital in 1925 and for months before and after.

My mother never helped me. When you were due she even sent for my sister Jessie to come back from her holiday with us because she needed her. The incident has always been a mystery to me. Your father was more angry about it than I had ever known him to be. Mrs Stein (wife of the Eastpark Church session clerk) came down to Rottenrow the day before I was due to get home. She brought all the necessary clothes for you, freshly washed and ironed and even had needle and thread so that she could alter a new bonnet, her present, if it didn't fit you. I have been blessed with wonderful friends.

(CM was born in Rottenrow Maternity Hospital, Glasgow, in June 1925. Because the birth was placenta praevia a Caesarian operation was necessary. It was thought surprising that both of us survived. The surgeon told Mother that she could have no more family, which was a disappointment to her. A hospital doctor said to a nurse, who reported it to Mother, that he had never seen any patient, not to mention someone suffering as Mother was, taking everything so calmly. Mother did not tell the nurse that she kept calm by reciting to herself Margaret Ogilvie's favourite Paraphrase, 'Art thou afraid His power shall fail?', Margaret Ogilvie being JM Barrie's semi-fictional mother in the book of that name. CM has a copy of the book, republished in 1925, presented to Helen MacLean, of Eastpark Church. The book was a UF Church of Scotland, Glasgow Presbytery, Welfare of Youth Examination Prize. CM was to survive not only the encounters with Annie but also a tracheotomy operation for diphtheria in Ruchhill Hospital at the age of three)

What a year 1928 was (Mother was to write more than 30 years later). Five of you down with diphtheria and your father with boils. It went on from March to October. I mustn't get like your Auntie Jessie who seems to remember only the hours when the sun didn't shine. I remember a minister's wife in Alness who went to the doctor because she felt so exhausted etc. He said to her, 'There's nothing the matter with you except that you're a tired wifie. That's quite plenty.'

Florrie went to Killearnan with us on holiday and was like one of the family. She wasn't really a servant but deserves to be mentioned honourably and with gratitude. She is now a Health Welfare visitor in Hamilton. She couldn't be asked to undertake the heavier kind of housework. Mrs B did that and was with us if I remember rightly up to the time that we left Glasgow.

Mrs B was a cheery little body with an almost Mongolian cast of features, and she was the most typical Mrs Mop of any that I had met. Annie, with the unaccountableness of everything about her, spoke well and without a pronounced accent. Mrs A and Nellie were just ordinary Glasgow, but Mrs B was often unintelligible. She said 'yous' for 'you', called children and sometimes grown-ups 'hens', and the construction of her sentences was incredibly involved. She used to annoy Florrie very much by calling her Florrah, and for a long time we quoted her when accidents happened. She broke things often and grieved over them but there was never any suggestion of replacing them. One day when she had been more ham-handed than usual, she came down to the kitchen with the third of her breakages in her hand – a bedroom utensil – sat down heavily in a chair and wailed, 'This is my unlucky day Florrah.' She had another little trick that shocked Florrie's Highland pride. If what she got to eat – and she took the maximum number of meals in the house – happened to be portable she wrapped it in paper and took it home for Maria's supper. Maria was a daughter who lived with her. She had also a married daughter, who had two little boys. It was from some reference to these two boys that I learnt that 'folk like us', to quote Mrs B, didn't give their boys overcoats. That would be aping their betters and make them unpopular amongst their neighbours.

The daughter also went out charring but her mother thought

she didn't need to do so, and was extravagant in her habits. 'She makes a fuss about being too fat,' she said, 'but it's nothing for her to eat half a pound of chocolate biscuits with her forenoon fly cup'. She told me a dreadful story one day about a neighbour's small child who had been sitting near the fire in a small chair when a 'flan' came down the chimney and burnt it so severely that it died. I was shocked and distressed and said so, whereupon Mrs B said cheerily, 'Oh, it was all right! She got £60 compensation.' She worked certain afternoons for two sisters, teachers whose activities filled her with amazement and awe. She retailed to me bits of conversations about theatres and concerts and lectures with wonder that anybody would be bothered. Her own entertainment consisted of going to a picture house on the Maryhill Road every Monday. All the women in Maryhill, she said, went to the pictures on Monday night, to get a rest after the washing. One of the lady teachers had been reading to the other one afternoon in Mrs B's presence a poem which struck her as being so strange that she asked what it was about. It was '*The Hound of Heaven*' and some effort had been made to explain it to her but her only reaction was to say to me, 'Isn't that terrible? Fancy calling God a dog!' When she left us it was to go as housekeeper to a policeman whose wife had died leaving two small boys. She wouldn't have been my choice for the job, but after we had gone to Dingwall they called on us one day and the boys looked happy and well cared for. She and they had been spending a holiday with the policeman's mother somewhere in Wester Ross and they were waiting in Dingwall for a train.

We moved to Dingwall in 1930. It's always a queer feeling to be making a round of last-for-the-present kind of visits. I've done it quite a number of times and always found it necessary to detach the mind, not being one of the people who can wallow in sentimental thoughts without being prostrated. My mother used to be able to make remarks like, 'What music in a mother's ears!', drop a tear or two and go on from there.

I look around my memory (Mother wrote this in 1963 at the time of the Profumo scandal) at the people who have meant much to me. How privileged and sheltered my life has been. My own father, your father and his friends, Mr Cable, Mr Bisset – countless more. Never having so far as I know met people of the Ward, Astor type what bothers me is this – would one guess at their shoddiness? I suppose it would work both ways. I would be as unattractive to them as they would be to me.

The time would fail me to tell of the host of people who time and again ministered voluntarily to our necessities. The Steins and Campbells provided a second home for you all, Miss Bain sewed for us, Mrs Urquhart came morning and evening to attend to you for weeks after I brought you home from the hospital, and last but not least Mrs James Hope. She took Barbara, Isabel and you almost daily to the Tannic-bo Gardens, as Barbara called them. She took you for afternoons to her house where she grossly overfed you, and was so fond of us all that when we left Glasgow she said she wouldn't have minded so much if she could only have gone and looked at our graves in Killermont.

11

NURSE ISABELLA GRANT (1852–1944)

(Mother's story of Nurse Grant falls mainly outside that of my parents' partnership, but Nurse Grant was very closely a part of Mother's family, and she came back into Mother's life after Father died. The story extends from mid-19th to mid-20th century and tells of a character who belonged peculiarly to her time and setting. I remember Nurse Grant clearly and can still hear her voice and taste the awful cake she brought as a gift when she joined us on Christmas Days in Aberdeen. I was abroad in the Services when she died. She was buried in a grave that let her maintain her Christian sense of thrift, though perhaps not of propriety.)

My recollections of Nurse Grant (Mother wrote) go back as far as memory itself. She was always in the background of our family life as a kind of benevolent aunt. My mother had more confidence in her than in any of her own sisters. When I was a child Nurse Grant visited us once a year and usually stayed for a few days. She seemed very grand, tall and heavily built, and dressed in a silver-grey uniform – probably a 'best' one, it was made of silk lustre. She always wore a gold watch tucked into a watch-pocket at her waist, and attached to a long gold chain round her neck. She was at that time doing private nursing in the north of England. One summer she brought Jessie A and me handkerchief sachets, made by herself of white linen with a drawn threadwork pattern. One was lined with pale blue silk and the other with pink. They were our first personal possessions and we thought them wonderful. Actually they were very pretty and, along with nightdress bags of the same pattern which she gave us the following year, they were still in use when we were grown up.

I learnt a good deal about her early life from herself when she spent the last year of her life in our house (at Craighead,

Nurse Isabella Grant (1852–1944)

Banchory Devenick). She was born near Ellon and except that her mother was unmarried and lived on a farm, or worked on one, I know nothing of her background. She had practically no schooling and helped about the farm as soon as she could lift a potato or run a message. At the age of eleven she went to be servant to two old ladies. They were kind, good women, taught her carefully to do household tasks and to sew and knit, and instructed her in the Scriptures. Her wage was £1 in the half year but she never handled the money. It was put into a bankbook and carefully kept till she was considered ready to go into service in Aberdeen.

I don't know how old she was then, but by the time she was about 20 she was with the Abernethys at Ferryhill House and was as fortunately situated there as with the two old ladies at Ellon. She attended Melville Free Church which was then in Correction Wynd, and it was at the Bible Class there that my mother first met her. The Class was conducted by the Mr Collie for whose parents my mother worked in her early years in Aberdeen. My mother thought him the embodiment of all the Christian virtues. He was in fact a very fine man and an eminent preacher. In my first summer in Nethybridge we made the acquaintance of a family called Jackson who were members of his congregation in Birkenhead. One of the sons of this family was then preparing to go abroad as a medical missionary – Dr Arthur Jackson who died in Manchuria of bubonic plague in 1911. My copy of his biography has a letter from his mother pasted inside the cover.

I don't know when it was or why that a few years later, perhaps when Mr Collie left Aberdeen, at least three members of the Bible Class joined Crown Terrace Baptist Church – my mother, Isa Grant, and Katie Cocker, who became Mrs Cruickshank and then Mrs Boddie. They remained intimate friends all their lives. My mother went back to the Free Church with my father but it was because of her Baptist indoctrination that none of us was baptised.

It must have been soon after this that Isa Grant started nursing at the old Infirmary in Woolmanhill. It was a Spartan life. The food they got was incredibly poor and scarce, and there was no off-time. They got off on Sunday for either forenoon or evening church, and they were free to go out for a couple of hours after the day's work was done, but there was no half-day, and as for a whole day – she used to hold up her hands in amazement to hear of such a thing. When I remember her she was doing private nursing, and she had photos of patients, and pieces of jewellery that she got from them. She had a beautiful brooch that the Duchess of Northumberland gave her, but it was never possible to get her to speak about the places she had nursed in – she just wasn't interested in grand people.

I think she was completely lacking in aesthetic sense. She was looking through a bundle of photographs one day and I noticed one of a very beautiful girl and asked who she was. 'Oh,' she said, 'that was a young lady I nursed for a long time. She married and went to India. She used to write me and she sent me a white silk shawl'. I remarked that she was handsome and she said, 'Maybe she was. I never noticed.' She had a benevolent regard for most people but had so little to say about their appearance or manners that I was quite taken aback one day when Sir Thomas Mitchell (Lord Provost of Aberdeen) was mentioned. She knew him well because as a member of the Town Council he went a good deal about Oldmill Hospital, and his second wife is or was Dr Helen Innes who was resident there. I said I was surprised that she married him and she said, 'He's a very attractive little man.'

The inscription on her clock gives 1901 as the date of her leaving the Newcastle Association of Private Nurses, but she didn't retire then. She came to Aberdeen because her mother was getting old and she felt it her duty to be near her. By this time her mother lived somewhere near the Bridge of Don. My mother had never seen her and didn't even know her name. Isa had no affection for her but a strong sense of duty. Probably my mother or my brother Charlie would have held first place in her affections. She could never see a fault in him, thought him very amusing and could always find excuses for his misdeeds.

She took a post as Matron in the Infirmary part of the Poorhouse which was then in Nelson Street. She used to ask me down to sing to the patients. My mother wasn't enthusiastic but didn't like to refuse to let me; not that she objected to my going to sing but because the district round Nelson Street wasn't highly spoken of. There was an odd bearded chaplain there, Rev

Nurse Isabella Grant (1852–1944)

John Mackay – very unromantic, but Nurse Grant used to tease me about him. It pains me to think how brash I must have been, but I must have been very young, because the Poorhouse had been moved up to Oldmill by the time I was in College and went there with parties of students.

When her mother died, about 1907, Isa retired from nursing, took a flat in Rose Street and devoted all her time to Church and Mission work. A patient who was knowledgeable about money matters had invested her money for her, mostly in Armour's the bridge builders, and she considered that she could afford to retire. She was thrifty beyond the wildest dreams – not that she was greedy or mean, but so that she could give. It was her consuming passion. Unfortunately she couldn't bear to see what she thought of as extravagance in other people.

Katie Cocker asked her to keep house for her for a week – probably when she was on her honeymoon with Sam Boddie. There were three young Cruickshanks, contemporaries of ours, Alick, Eliza and Katie. Mr Cruickshank had left a lot of money and their standard of living was lavish in our estimation but wildly extravagant in Nurse Grant's. On the Sunday morning Eliza told her that they were accustomed to having ham and eggs for breakfast, but she utterly refused to countenance such waste – ham or eggs but not both.

On Saturday nights when perishable food was being sold off for next to nothing she made her purchases in the Aberdeen New Market. One of her favourites was 6d of cod which she cooked with flour to make a kind of shape. A slice per day as long as it lasted sufficed for her dinner. When she made tea she poured every drop out of the teapot and reheated it. She even brought home the left-over tea from social meetings: she was tea-maker in chief. Once when she had a supply of social-meeting tea she invited my mother and me to tea. She might have known better. My mother took one sip of her tea, realised where it had come from and after much talk said she wanted a drink of water and emptied her cup into the sink. If Nurse G noticed she said nothing but there were no more tea parties for us. She came to tea in my parents' house once a week and she always had her Christmas dinner with us. She was very independent and often brought buns. When my brothers came to their tea and saw that she was in the house they carefully avoided everything but plain

143

bread knowing that she patronised all the shops that produced quantity rather than quality.

When she returned to Aberdeen she joined Gilcomston Park Baptist Church and devoted all her time and energy and money to its activities. The war brought her some financial prosperity – Armours' paid huge dividends and bonuses. But she unwisely re-invested her surplus money in the firm and in 1919 it went bankrupt. She was then really poor till her banker insisted that she apply for the old age pension. She also had a Nurses' Pension of about £60.

My mother regarded some of her activities with serious disapproval – for instance she was one of a band of reformers who visited public houses on Saturday nights. I can't imagine what happened when they found themselves in the pub. Your Auntie J says they delivered tracts, but my impression is that they tried to induce men to go home before they had spent all their money, and my reason for this belief is that she once told me a curious story. I wish I could remember it more fully. There was a youngish man, much given to drink, whose wife was known to Isa. She gave him special attention, accompanied him home and talked to him for his good. She belonged to a generation that took the command 'to rebuke and exhort' quite literally. In course of time peace and order were restored to the home and a baby girl was born and named Isabella Grant. She kept a kindly eye on the family and when the girl married and left the town she presented her with a block of shares (she was still well-off at the time) and said farewell. She hadn't cared much for the young woman who bore her name and felt that she had now completed her responsibility for her.

When she first retired from nursing she took to wearing ordinary clothes, but she had no dress sense and was so unfamiliar-looking that my mother suggested she should continue to wear nurse's uniform because it suited her and would be thriftier. She told me that she got her last new dress for my marriage. That was in 1910; she died in 1944, so she hadn't been extravagant.

Nurse G discovered during her rounds of visits that a little girl was unable to go to the Sunday School picnic for want of a dress. She remembered that she had a piece of dark red cord silk and promised that she would supply the dress. Accordingly she set to, made the dress with a yoke, as was then the fashion, and put lace round the neck. But alas! the yoke was too small and the dress didn't fit; history doesn't say what the little girl felt, but Nurse G's disappointment was bitter – it was such lovely stiff silk. However, the child mustn't suffer, so she went to Raggie Morrison's, bought print at fourpence halfpenny per yard and made another frock – no doubt infinitely more suitable.

To explain why she had so much stock at her disposal, I must tell you that one of her chief social services – all voluntary and often thankless – was to nurse old people who were living alone and too poor to afford help. Most, probably all of them, were people she had known for years. When they died she saw to everything, arranged for the funeral and divided their scanty belongings as she thought fit. We were often told about how so and so had had a nice blanket which somebody else was glad to get. Anything that was likely to be useful she laid past till she found a place for it – thus the stiff red silk.

There were two young people, a lad and a girl whose families belonged to Gilcomston Park Church. Both of them were victims of some childhood illness – probably polio though nobody had then heard the name. The lad had a withered arm and the girl was slightly lame; both were also a little sub-normal mentally, but not very noticeably so. They wanted to get married but their families were very poor, couldn't do anything to help them, and could see little prospect of their helping themselves. Nurse Grant's heart bled for them. Her negotiations took a long time and were much talked of. She got no encouragement at our house, though we knew nothing of the young couple, but in course of time they got married. Nurse G bought material and made the wedding dress, had the wedding feast in her own house, and had previously found a room for them at the top of one of these high tenements in Crown Street. The husband, when he did anything, sold kindling wood from door to door. In course of time – quite a long time – they had a child, a girl who was perfectly normal, in fact she was reported to be very intelligent.

By the time this child was ten or eleven years old the wife's parents had died and Nurse G was still adviser in chief. One day Mrs – I never knew the name – arrived in Rose Street in a great state of excitement. She had had a letter from a lawyer in the

North of England to say that her mother's sister had died and left her all her money, and suggesting that she come to Leeds or Hull, I can't remember which, and decide what was to be done about the estate. Once more Nurse G stepped in, supplied money for the fares and saw to things generally.

It was several years before they returned to Aberdeen. The aunt had married a clothier who had a small business. There had been the minimum of communication between the families and they knew little about them except that their only child had died. The clothier had developed his business into what was then called a 'shilling-a-week' affair and prospered enormously. He predeceased his wife and when she died the fortune came to the niece in Aberdeen. It amounted to something like £20,000. The couple, on being consulted about the business, decided that they would carry it on themselves, with disastrous results, but they had still enough left to buy a bungalow in Aberdeen and live comfortably.

They didn't return to Gilcomston Park Church but Nurse G met the woman and got their address and an invitation to visit them some day. She went, rang the bell and got no reply. She saw that someone came to the window and looked out, but still nobody opened the door so she turned away. Some time after, she saw the man in Rosemount Viaduct but was pretty sure that he looked into a shop window to avoid her. She spoke to him, said that she had called at the house and got no reply. She thought him evasive and shifty but was unwilling to believe that anything more than his natural want of wit was indicated. She didn't however repeat her visit and one day she saw the family in the distance, saw that when they recognised her they crossed the street. On that bleak note the story finishes.

When we returned to Aberdeen in 1932 Nurse Grant came back to the family like one who was returning home. She had her Christmas dinner with us, even after we went out to Banchory-Devenick. When she felt that she would soon be unable to live alone she told me one day that she wouldn't like to go into an old people's home, but would make up her mind to be contented in it if she had to go, and I said I wouldn't see her at a loss. That was why she said to Dr Grieve when he forbade her to keep on her house that she thought I would look after her. He came out to Craighead and asked if I had really meant that I would give her a home. It so happened that I was likely to be a good deal alone too and I willingly agreed to take her.

She wanted to give me all her furniture but there was no room for it, so she gave most of it away and brought only the furniture for her own room so that she would feel at home in it. She also gave away all her jewellery rather than put it in her will. She had already given her last £100 to Gilcomston Park Church, reckoning that she had enough in the bank to pay for her funeral and that her £60 nurse's pension and her old age pension of 10s a week would provide for all her necessities.

At 89 she was still fairly active, had her breakfast in bed but was up from 10 am till 7 pm, tidied her room and went for walks and was very careful not to intrude on the family. She had her meals with me except when there were visitors. She didn't hear well and was embarrassed in company. It was then she told me all her history and gave me character sketches of a lot of the people she had worked amongst in the church. The church people came frequently to see her but she wasn't always very pleased to see them. She thought, poor soul, that some of them hadn't treated her well. The fact was that she had outstayed her usefulness. A very nice couple, Mr and Mrs Wilson, had undertaken, at her request, to take charge of her money affairs and Mrs W called often and used to confide in me about how glad they were when she left the town and had to give up making the tea at the Guild. She never allowed them to have anything but large baps with their tea, and she wouldn't use anything but the cheapest tea. The minister who had been in Gilcomston Park when she came back to Aberdeen was Rev Grant Gibb. He was a bachelor and his sister lived with him. They were very friendly with Nurse Grant and appreciated her work and her generosity. But Grant Gibb retired and a young minister came who didn't see why a woman who was nearer 90 than 80 should be the ruling spirit in the congregation. Without saying a word to her he appointed a friend of his own to superintend the baptismal services. She was very sore about this and wept every time she thought of it. Evidently it was her duty and pleasure to see to it that when girls were to be baptised they were provided with the right kind of robes. Often she provided them at her own expense. She also gave them tea after the baptism, and I suppose it was natural that she hadn't realised she was too old.

That minister didn't stay long and a Mr Turnbull came in his place. He was most attentive, came every fortnight to see her and did everything he possibly could to help her. He discovered that she had difficulty with the small print in her Bible and got a strong magnifying glass for her. That was no use because her hand trembled when she held it, so he got one of his members who was in Whitelaws to design and make a stand into which she could fit the glass and move the Bible below it. It was a most ingenious affair and perfect for the purpose but she refused to use it until she had paid for it. It was a gift but she would have none of it. After a good deal of persuasion she told me that she wouldn't accept a gift from that man. He had insulted her beyond all possibility of forgiveness. It seemed that some time before she came out to Craighead Dr Grieve had advised her to go to Whitelaws and get a belt for hernia. The belt didn't fit, indeed it hurt her, and she went back to get it altered. The woman who had fitted it was rude and said, 'There's nothing wrong with it. Mr . . . said you were a fashious old thing and nothing would please you.' She left the shop without another word and had never mentioned the incident to anybody, but she couldn't accept a present from Mr . . . She had known him all his life, she said, and had been very kind to his widowed mother. I tried to persuade her that he probably never said any such thing and that the woman should have been reported to the management, but she insisted on giving Mr Turnbull 10s, which the man refused to take and put into the church funds.

Speaking of Mr Turnbull reminds me that one day he brought his little girl out with him. I took charge of her whilst he visited with Nurse Grant and we went up to look at the hens. Eggs were as scarce as money – it was wartime – and she was thrilled to take four eggs, one for each of them, out of the nest. She ran in to show them to her father and Nurse Grant, and while he thanked me Nurse Grant kept silent. After they had gone she said it was really unnecessary for me to have given away eggs and especially fresh eggs. It was no use to point out that eggs weren't worth giving unless they were fresh. She kept on saying that really, to give away fresh eggs . . .!!

She didn't always give cheap things either. Although a stern teetotaller all her life she had for a great many years given a friend, Mrs Brewster who was a semi-invalid, a bottle of port for her birthday. She bought it always from the grocer at the corner of Summer Street and Huntly Street and it amused her that on the last occasion the grocer had said he couldn't sell it to her in the shop, out of hours, but if she would go and wait in the back lane he would bring it out to her.

She had no fault to find with her lodgings at Craighead so far as I know except that the food was too rich and she was putting on weight. She liked milk puddings but it horrified her that I made mine with ordinary milk. She had always bought skim-milk for hers and added water to it after that.

She contributed to every imaginable mission and charity. When I went to collect her pension I had to buy dozens of stamps for her. Then she sent 1s worth to as many places as she could afford at the moment. I'm sorry to say that I was interfering enough to point out that she was giving a disproportionate amount of money to the Post Office but she couldn't and wouldn't understand that. She probably started that method of distribution to keep in personal touch and perhaps to get postal packets. She got all kinds of little magazines and pamphlets.

She had been with us for nearly a year when Mr and Mrs Wilson came out for her to give her a day in town and take her to visit her friends. She was away from mid-forenoon till 9 at night – far too long a day for her – and she had visited an incredible number of people. When she came home she was so tired that she had to be helped to undress, and she was very cross with me because when I took off her boots I took out the 'pints' (laces), She lived for about six weeks after that but was always confused and difficult, and when she took a shock was only six days in a nursing home.

Mr Wilson had had no instructions about her funeral; and wondered where her mother was buried, but she had told me that she was to be buried in Nellfield. She had gone to Springfield to buy a grave for herself but found that it was to cost so much that she couldn't bring herself to part with the money. A friend who lived in Cairncry then told her that she had the deeds, or whatever the word is, for a grave in Nellfield, that she wouldn't need that grave because she would be buried with her husband, and Nurse G might have it if she so wished. I remembered the lady's name and address, though I have forgotten them both now, and Mr Wilson arranged accordingly.

The funeral was from Gilcomston Park. Mr Grant Gibb took the service, and the whole congregation filed past the coffin to take a last look at her as if she had been royalty. I went from the church to the cemetery in the same car as Grant Gibb and his sister. He said I had been very kind and that the Lord had wonderfully provided for dear Nurse Grant, but his pious words were received without enthusiasm. I knew that he had phoned Mr Wilson to send a taxi for them, to be paid out of 'the estate'. The Gibbs were wealthy people and lived in Queen's Road on the car route.

After the service at the grave a lady came up to me and said, 'I think you must be Mrs MacLean,' and proceeded to tell me that she was the friend to whom the grave belonged. Her brother was buried in it and as he had never married there was nobody else to occupy it. I immediately had a most irreverent picture of the mutual surprise of the bachelor brother and Nurse Grant if the old fashioned ideas of a resurrection morning should turn out to be true.

The 'estate' didn't need much winding up. Mr and Mrs Wilson accompanied me home, at my request, to look through such possessions as were left. She had directed that all her clothes be sent to Quarriers Homes. The dress that had been new 34 years earlier wasn't amongst them and Mr W went into town for some sacks, bundled everything into them and sold them as rags. It took most of the £60 that was left in the bank to clear up the nursing home and funeral expenses. Dr Grieve refused payment. He had been as kind to Nurse Grant as if she had been his mother, said it had been his great privilege and he wouldn't dream of taking money for it. The residue of her estate was to be divided between the Regions Beyond Mission and the Mildmay Mission to the Jews. They got about £10 each.

The furniture that she brought out to Craighead was of course mine. Some of it I still have. You have her table.

POSTSCRIPT

COLIN MACLEAN

In the spring of 1932 my father had been minister of Castle Street Church, Dingwall, for two years. He arranged to spend some time in Orkney, hoping this would improve the state of his health, which had deteriorated seriously in the later years of his ten-year ministry at East Park Church, Glasgow. His visit to Orkney was postponed because he was invited, though not a Commissioner, to join in the Highland Night at the General Assembly of the Church of Scotland and to deliver an address to the Assembly on the work of the Church's Highland Committee. On Saturday 28 May he spoke to the Commissioners: an attractively printed copy of the speech was preserved by my mother and is in my keeping. Father returned to Dingwall to conduct the morning service in his church on the 29th. In the afternoon, again in his church, he took part in a mass meeting of local youth organisations, at which he gave the address.

At this service I sat, not in the manse pew but, as I remember, crowded into a back corner seat feeling lonely in the packed church. At one point the assembled forces joined in reciting the Lord's Prayer. My father did not normally lead his congregation in recitation of the Lord's Prayer, or of anything else. No ritual collect in his order of service. I was astonished and alarmed by the sudden surge of noise. I went home to say it had sounded like lions roaring.

Father felt unwell on the Sunday and became much worse on the Monday. An acute form of septic enteritis was diagnosed. He died on the Thursday of the following week. There was a funeral service four days later in Castle Street Church, and then Father was laid to rest in Cromarty beside his first son, Alasdair, who had died as a baby sixteen years earlier when Father was minister at the United Free Church there.

Your Father and I

The North Star of 11 June and *The Northern Chronicle* of 15 June carried lengthy obituaries and tributes. *The Highland News* of 11 June reported, among other things, that Father had been 'in wide demand as a preacher at Communion seasons throughout the Highlands'. *The British Weekly* of 16 June included a tribute. The *Ross-shire Journal* of 17 June gave two and a half columns to appreciation and tributes, to the details of events leading up to Father's death and to accounts of the funeral service and burial, concluding with a list of pall-bearers, who included my brother Roderick (then aged 14), my three uncles, two minister cousins of my father, and the session clerks of Castle Street and East Park churches.

In the evening on the Monday of the funeral, I went with my mother in a car to Cromarty to see the grave. I don't know who was driving nor do I remember whether other members of the family accompanied us. At some stage before the funeral my mother had taken me into an upstairs front bedroom of the Dingwall manse in Achany Road to see the closed coffin in which my father lay. She had rebelled against the practice of encouraging people, old or young, to view the remains. So I saw only the coffin, and then I saw the grave.

I have a clear picture of my father in only two memories. The first – my earliest memory, I think – was when I was three, on a Sunday morning around mid-day in 1928. I was being rushed to Glasgow's Ruchill Hospital where I was to undergo the tracheotomy operation for diphtheria. I was being carried into an ambulance outside the Manse in Lansdowne Crescent. I looked back and saw my father just returning from morning service. He wore a shiny black top-hat. My second clear memory of Father is of standing at the Manse gate in Dingwall one evening with some other children and watching my mother and father returning from a walk. As usual he carried a walking stick (probably the one that figures in the story of his puzzling legacy) and he swung it on every second step in a way that I find myself doing.

Probably when I was five, the family had a holiday in Contin, where there was a bobbin-mill along the road from the family cottage. Father delighted me immensely by using bobbins – I cannot imagine how – to make a small 'cartie' for me, which I sat on while he pulled it. My memory is principally of the pleasure rather than of my father, who of course was there but I don't see him: he was high above me as I sat proudly on the little wooden vehicle. Neither have I any clear picture of Father at home or in the pulpit, though I remember clearly that he presided at family prayers in Achany Road after tea-time: on my knees, I pressed my face into a large leather armchair – of which the smell is still sharp in my nostrils. He was there in the room behind me as I knelt. It was only a few days after my seventh birthday that Father died, but he has held a dominant place in my life.

The *Ross-shire Journal* records an astonishing array of facts and impressions about my father. For me the most striking – and indeed sensitive – part of the report is in an account of the address given by the Rev Roderick Fraser, of St Clement's, Dingwall, on the Sunday morning after my father died. He had been with my mother as my father was dying. We must, he said, bow our hearts to God's will and believe, as Mrs MacLean 'so beautifully put it, on Thursday night, when we waited for the last – "The King has need of him" '.

That style of thinking, that level of reverence for reverends, that talent for ready biblical allusion, that proportion of press attention to church affairs – all of these belong to an era that seems distanced by much more than six decades, but they account in large part for the fact that his family continued to live very much in his shadow. Though I as the youngest had known him least, I was a lot in my mother's company and if we were out together I could always tell from the way she gripped my hand if she was thinking about Father. Clearest among such memories is of a summer evening when I had accompanied her to hear the great JS Stewart, then minister of Beechgrove Church in Aberdeen. The last hymn was 'The Day Thou Gavest' and I then had – for a young boy – the uneasy task of accompanying her up Mid Stocket Road, back to our new home in Harcourt Road. Great preaching always moved her to tears, especially if she could say, 'It reminded me of Alick's preaching'. She gripped my hand tightly.

She would talk to me as she talked to all of the family and to many friends, in a relaxed way about sermons, their themes, their import etc. Her letters in later years were just the same, and church affairs and church history, or certain sectors of it, were constant topics. Such matters were, I suppose, as familiar to me as the identity of cars or the performance of football teams might now be to many boys. In 1935 or '36 – so I was ten or eleven years old – an HM Inspector visited Mile End Primary School in Aberdeen and came into our classroom. I now find it difficult to believe what I remember of his class inspection. After a few preliminaries he told the teacher he would take over the class. She stood back while he asked 'Can anyone tell me the date of the Disruption?' One hand went up – mine. 'Yes, sir, it was 1843,' He was rather amused. 'Oh? Do you know the name of the Moderator of the Church of Scotland?' 'Yes, sir, it's Lang.' 'Ah, and do you know the name of the Archbishop of Canterbury?' 'Yes, sir, it's Lang too,' (They were brothers). My recollection is that he turned approvingly to the teacher, made his farewells, and for a dream's brief while I was in favour with her – though of course she had taught me none of those facts of church life. What HM Inspector today would approach a class thus? What child today etc?

Mother took me to one service which brought no tears to her eyes. She recalls it in her account of the Gordon Mission. Soon after we arrived in Aberdeen in 1932 it was impressed upon Mother that she should renew her acquaintance with the Gordon Mission, then under the direction of her Uncle John who lived at 178 Mid Stocket Road with her three formidable aunts Isa, Lizzie and Jessie – the last a teacher at Mile End School. Mother's Uncle James (JA) had died in 1926. A visiting evangelist was preaching at the Mission. The Mission Hall was almost full when we arrived, so that I was placed in one vacant space at the end of a bench towards the back while Mother was ushered to a seat nearer the front. As the evangelist waxed more and more eloquent he warmed to a hell-fire theme which, as I found later, made my mother increasingly alarmed about the effect this might have on me, unseen by her, at the back of the dark hall. She remembered how such preaching had disturbed her sister Jessie as a child. Also she was angry at having been cornered by family pressures into this awkward situation. Actually I found hell-fire then, as I find it now, at best entertaining and at worst rather ludicrous. That evening's experience probably inoculated me for ever against such lurid threats. I think, too, it helped make me aware of and sensitive to the art – and the abuse – of eloquence.

The family's return to Aberdeen was in some respects a mistake: relatives in proximity can be a mixed blessing. The best argument was that my sister Helen was by then a student there. As Mother makes clear, Father had not believed that a minister should lay up worldly goods. By the time all accounts to tradesmen had been paid (£95 12s 11d), bank overdraft cleared (£10 11s 10d) etc, from his Equitable Life Assurance Policy for £160 a balance of £53 10s 5d was paid to Mother by the Dingwall solicitors Duncan & Duncan. Mr Robert Stein, who had been session clerk at East Park, and Mr Arthur Duncan for the Dingwall congregation, organised a collection of money from the four congregations which Father had served, also from Dingwall district and from some church trusts. The total collected was £592 15s 3d. They also organised the funding of the impressive gravestone at Cromarty – which by now bears the names of my father, mother, two brothers and two sisters. Mother found enough for a payment of £600 towards the cost of a newly-built semi-detached house in Harcourt Road, on the outskirts of Aberdeen. She took out a bond for the remaining £500, the annual interest payment for which was a recurring nightmare to her. The advantage of the Harcourt Road house compared with others she had considered was that it had four bedrooms, one of them a small attic room which for some time my brother and I were to share.

The manse furniture was tragically inappropriate for our new house. Planning for the move must have been hurried and unthought. One large beautifully curved mahogany side-table which had graced the hallway in Achany Road could not be manoeuvred through the front door at Harcourt Road and stood for a day or two in the summer sun on the rubble-strewn patch of ground that was to be our front garden. I don't know who took it away.

Mother had a minister's widow's pension and also a church pension for the two of us who were under 12 years of age. Her total income, she recalled many years later, was £98 in the half year for six of us – often seven, for her sister Jessie was with us a lot. I think she must have had money from some trust other than the pensions which I remember as £72 for her and £36 each for my sister, Isabel, and myself – though Isabel's £36 would have ceased by 1934. In 21 Harcourt Road we were only a stone's throw from 178 Mid Stocket Road where Mother's three aunts and their brother John lived. When we arrived in 1932 Uncle John broke his lifelong commitment to meanness by saying that he would each year provide me with a suit – from a tailor's shop near the foot of the Kirkgate, I remember. After a few years the price for the outfit soared above £1 to £1 2s 6d. Uncle John refused to pay more than £1 and his sisters told Mother the suits had become too expensive – 'in all the circumstances a strange reason,' Mother wrote, recalling that at the same time she had to find the money (12 shillings) for a second-hand sofa – it was covered with American cloth which flaked easily – required to replace a chaise-longue type of couch which had disintegrated, partly because I used it as a bus when neighbouring children came in to play.

Of those difficult days Mother wrote: 'The sad thing about being comfortably off is the difficulty about presents. I have seen days when anything, even a cake of soap, was a welcome gift. Any gift is welcome – I haven't the right word, but necessity sharpens gratitude. Auntie Isa once said to me, "I can't bear to think how poor we were at Midward". Your sister Helen has the same attitude. I am not allowed to refer to our hard-up days. For myself I like to think of the 23rd Psalm, "Thou preparest a table before me in the presence of mine enemies. My cup runneth over" as an expression of gratitude and not as a slap to other people, as CS Lewis apparently does.'

Mother's letters were to refer occasionally to the debts which she had amassed in the 1930s and '40s. She settled them all eventually by the mid-1950s. One or two had been generously converted to gifts. In 1960 she said in a letter that she had regarded it as a special Providence that all her creditors did not become insistent at the same moment. 'I had the Prince of Bankers,' she wrote, of a Mr Gibson (his daughter was in my class at Mile End School) who, amazingly, allowed Mother in the late 1930s to transfer to his bank the overdraft about which another bank manager had become unpleasantly impatient. I recall some Saturday morning visits as a boy alone to the bank with a cheque which Mother hoped Mr Gibson would cash. Each time the teller would retire to Mr Gibson's office for instruction. At least one time Mr Gibson came out, told the teller to give me the money, then said to me in a kindly voice that he'd like to see Mother as soon as she could manage to come to the bank.

A Miss Mackenzie in Dingwall left Mother £200 in the late 1930s. 'It was then,' Mother wrote 'that we got the Harcourt Road house painted, though to be sure the £200 just covered the overdraft so that I could start to run it up again.' The Harcourt Road house had to be sold in 1940 – not a good year for selling a house – so that pressing debts could be met. We then moved to a rented house, Craighead, Banchory Devenick, a mile or so beyond the Old Bridge of Dee. Electricity had not by then reached that corner of Kincardineshire so cooking was on a range fire. We purchased an Aladdin lamp and a Tilley lamp as well as a large supply of candles, the last much in use when paraffin for the lamps was not available – usually because of wartime shortage of supplies. For our fires we were allowed to collect fallen branches from the nearby wood. The move to the country was welcomed by the family, not least because local farms allowed us more than our allotted rations of eggs. For a short time we kept our own hens.

One day shortly before we left Aberdeen, Mother was walking homeward down Harcourt Road and saw there was a man waiting at her front door. She knew well he must be a creditor so she just turned away and went for a walk. In the 1970s I was invited to speak at the annual dinner of the Seven Incorporated Guilds in Aberdeen. I took the opportunity to say a belated thank you to all the tolerant tradesmen who had let Mother run up accounts which in some cases she took years to pay.

Mother wrote, 'I came across the remark that there are things one can't afford not to get. It's very true. Nobody who hasn't experienced real poverty can possibly understand the urge and the need to have a burst. Also there are times when appearances must be kept up. Morale demands it.' Responding to a letter from myself in which I mentioned money difficulties, she replied, 'When you speak of working out your financial state I'm like the woman in *Pilgrim's Progress* who "smiled while the water stood in her eyes". I used to add and subtract but mostly subtract night after night when I went to bed. Sometimes, now that I am not in money difficulties, I often count the money in my purse for no reason at all, just a silly kind of habit.'

Mother maintained a simple determination that we should

not be denied whatever education we would have had if Father had been alive. In the event, four of her family gained six degrees between them – all from Aberdeen University – and one daughter gained five nursing qualifications. It was partly Mother's determination to hold true to what she felt was owed to Father's memory that in turn made her the stronger light, or influence, with the family. As William Macleod in Cromarty said, 'She's no neen ahin himsel.' Her role was further strengthened by her becoming the teller of the family story. Much could be written about Mother herself and much is revealed about her in the many letters to which no reference is made in these pages. I have chosen to limit myself in the preceding account to what Mother wished to put on record about times and people which I as the youngest member of the family could not be expected to remember.

In her last years Mother looked back a lot, always with acceptance, often with gratitude. 'I wouldn't wish anything changed,' she wrote. 'Looking back over my 70 odd years I feel that they are best described in that verse of *The Sands of Time* that begins, "With mercy and with judgment my web of time He wove".' I have not been able to trace the poem. She was given to speak and write of the moments of pure joy in her youth in Aberdeen. One fond memory was of walking to church alone with her father, her hand in his, at one with him and happy: 'I can feel the straightness of my back,' she said, 'and the hardness of the backs of my legs.' Another was of meeting old Mr Cable, their neighbour, in the Victoria Park and getting an illustrated text from him – 'He took me to His banqueting house and His banner over me was love'. The memory she treasured most, she said, was of standing beside Father in the South Church, Aberdeen. He was in his chaplain's uniform, on leave from France. They were singing 'Fair waved the golden corn in Canaan's pleasant land'. She thought then that this would probably be for ever the happiest moment of her life.

Those moments recalled in the tranquillity of her late years were all of times long before 1932, the year my father died. Better to end her story there as she told it – in her large, confident handwriting over hundreds of sheets of blue writing paper.